Live Life to the Full

What I have learned from Paddling the Mekong to Skiing to the South Pole

An inspirational guide for living life to the full

Printed and bound in England by www.printondemand-worldwide.com

http://www.fast-print.net/bookshop

LIVE LIFE TO THE FULL
Copyright © Paula Reid 2016

A catalogue record for this book is available from the British Library

ISBN 978-178456-389-9

First published 2016 by
FASTPRINT PUBLISHING
Peterborough, England

Live Life to the Full

What I have learned from Paddling the Mekong to Skiing to the South Pole

An inspirational guide for living life to the full

By Paula Reid

Paula is on a mission: to live life to the full.

To enrich her life with adventures, achievements, experiences and wonder; seizing the day and savouring the moment.

Our lives can be vibrant, potent and enriched if we embrace the concept of living and engage with the world around us, even in small and simple ways – making the most of the gift of life. Paula's adventures help her to feel completely alive and know that when she draws her last breath, it will be with no regrets.

Paula Reid is a performance coach, inspirational speaker, adventurer and author of several books. Her list of goals ranges from massive expeditions to the mundane and bizarre: from skiing to the South Pole to swimming with sharks, from participating in the world bog snorkeling championships to buying a round of drinks for a pub full of strangers...

www.paulareid.com

Imagine... You are lying on your death bed watching your toes curl up and you're thinking, what have I done with my life?

You don't want to be thinking about all the things you could have done or should have done. So when you press the "Action Replay" button on your life, will it only contain images such as loading the dishwasher, watching TV and writing emails?

Or will it contain something more extraordinary and adventurous such as paddling the Mekong, sailing around the world or skiing to the South Pole?

We only live once and we're a long time dead. So lean in.

This book is dedicated to Kate Stainsby and her family; and Jon Scott and his family.

What other people are saying

Ms. Reid's coverage on how everyone should strive for their goals while challenging the barriers that they may face is quite encouraging, especially for women. Daily Tribune, Bahrain

She talks passionately about her extraordinary and sometime inexplicable need to take in as many new experiences as possible. Reader's Digest

Within minutes of setting foot inside Paula Reid's intriguing house she had thrust a penis gourd into my hand. It was an unusual welcome, but one totally in keeping with the character of this ebullient woman and her breath-taking, non-stop lifestyle. The News

Adventure lover Paula Reid has ticked off 108 items from her bucket list including climbing mountains, sailing around the world, skiing to the South Pole – and acting as an extra in a Hollywood film. Daily Star.

But seriously there is a much bigger picture. My life is way too comfortable and easy. I want – need – to see what I'm really made of. Do I really amount to anything much? If nothing else the Global Challenge is a massive kick up the backside. The Telegraph.

Paula is great! She's interesting, full of humor yet serious and knows how to connect & relate her personal story to business insights. Everyone was fascinated by her and told us it was both inspiring & interesting. Shira.

I heard you talk at our success day in Leeds last year. I was impressed by your talk... However, your book, OMG the best... book I've ever read. Thank you so much, I've learnt loads. You are without doubt a most clever insightful, thinker and writer... there is sooo much to think about! With gratitude and respect... Conference attendee

Absolutely fantastic. Very, very inspirational. [I] take away from it – focus, goal setting... determination... absolutely brilliant. Forever Living Products

What did I take from the book? Just don't quit. Just don't give up at all... really inspirational. Crawford.

It was absolutely brilliant! So inspirational. And it gave me some real thoughts about actually writing my list of things to do and then making them happen. Brilliant. Absolutely fantastic. Mike

I bought the book because I just want to find out more. It was a lovely, lovely inspirational talk and I really do take my hat off to her. Life is short and if you're not careful your dreams will have passed you by so you really have got to plan those challenges but then just get up and do them because otherwise time has gone. Tony

It was a really good presentation – we talked about it all the way back to the office! Definitely spurred me on to actually start planning my Kilimanjaro trip! Karen.

Great lessons from your experiences – "a big thumbs up" Specsavers.

You are a wonderful writer and you brought everything to life. I really enjoyed reading this. All I can say is that you are an amazing woman. And I hope that I do get the opportunity to meet you, Pauline

Contents

Diary Extract: Day 46. 5km from South Pole -40°C

I saw a coloured blob in the distance which gradually solidified into a yellow metal sign declaring 'Welcome to the South Pole.' Wow. Crazy. Such an amazing and longed-for sight yet we still had five kilometres to go.

It's not every day you get to ski in to the South Pole and Amundsen-Scott research station. We slowly skied forward on the frozen track. Ahead was a semi-circle of flags and a barber's pole with a mirror ball on top - the ceremonial South Pole - and an Amundsen-Scott sign and marker denoting the geographic South Pole.

My emotions were all over the place and my face was aching from trying not to cry.

Chapter 1
A Matter of Life and Death

I have a mission: to enrich my life with adventures, achievements, experiences, memories, wonder and magic before I die. Our lives can be vibrant, potent and intense if we embrace the concept of living; immerse ourselves in the world around us and engage whole-heartedly with our existence. This is what I call Living Life to the Full. It's about loving life; not just existing, nor being a passenger or a spectator, but being a fully involved, committed participant. I want to engross myself in the opulent richness that life gifts us. The richness of our amazing planet – its countries, geographies, weather and nature; the richness of the people on it – the variety, eccentricities, stories and talents; the richness of me – what I am capable of, what I can achieve when I really push myself, what it feels like to climb a mountain peak, jump out of a plane or arrive at the South Pole after skiing for 46 days.

I'm not talking about doing everything to the MAX. It's not about a continuous striving, a relentless agitation or an addiction to adrenaline; it's not about screaming and shouting along a never-ending rollercoaster of tough challenges and extreme experiences. I happen to enjoy those too, but living life to the full is about being fully alive – whatever that means to you – and includes the small stuff and being fully present. It means having time to stop and stare, notice and engage, be curious and childlike; absorbing and savouring this incredible thing we call "life."

I had a friend called Kate who was vibrant and vital, physically fit and very lively, who threw herself into activities and laughed with all her heart. I met her in July 2004 when I first joined my team for the Global Challenge round-the-world yacht race. She was already on the team and took me under her wing as we had the same technical role and responsibilities during the race. We were assigned to each other officially as "crew buddies" which meant that we looked after each other's well-being, and unofficially we were drinking allies in port, legendary with the others crews for helping them drink through their corporate-sponsored booze budgets! We were two of a kind - active, fun loving and sociable - and we got on very well; she was a warm and gregarious friend.

Eight years later, on New Year's Day, she died when she capsized in her kayak. She was 42, newly married and mother to a little boy.

At her funeral, a friend from her anti-natal class spoke about the times that she, Kate and other new mothers got together at each other's houses for coffee and catch ups with babies and toddlers in tow. The house they chose to meet at inevitably turned into an explosion of mayhem and debris caused by the combination of mothers, babies and toddlers doing what they do. One of the mothers couldn't abide it when it was her turn to host. She stressed about the chaos, cleaning up all the time they were there and grumbling about it for days afterwards. One day Kate decided to share with her a piece of wisdom: "**Embrace the Mess**."

In the eulogy, the friend acknowledged that Kate was too young to die. That this death was unnaturally early, that it was unjust for someone so vibrant, with a new husband and a young child, to die. She went on to suggest that we all "Embrace the Mess" that was Kate's passing. We had to accept that she had left us and enfold Kate's story into our hearts. By now my tears were running unchecked, thinking about Kate, crying/laughing at the story and moved by the clever analogy. It was an insightful and poignant piece of wisdom that made us sit up, pull ourselves together and force a shaky smile. Life sometimes presents us with situations that are hard to understand and hard to swallow. I was grievously pained by Kate's death. I was uncomfortable to be at a funeral for someone who was young and living life to the full, but we do only live once and we should embrace the mess that is life and we should embrace the mess that is death, even a young death. We never know how long our one precious life is going to last. It is a pity that sometimes we need this mortal perspective - this "dead-line" - to remind us to live.

I like to embrace the mess that is living, knowing that the mess of dying is inexorably to come, and not wanting to die having not fully lived. I don't want to be lying on my deathbed regretting all the things I haven't done or even all the crazy things that I have done. Life needn't be a controlled and comfortable journey on a well-worn highway from the cradle to the grave. Life is an adventure, an exciting, stretchy experience full of discovery and surprises; fickle, chancy and uncertain. Life is an incredible gift and I believe in making the most of it - living life to the full for at least these reasons:

− The newness, change and variety expand my experience, enriching my understanding; broadening and opening my mind to other worlds and ways. Living life to the full is about exploration, learning and discovery
− I feel more alive, alert, stimulated, in the moment, sharp, fully focused, and fully present
− Motivation and inspiration
− It pushes, stretches and challenges me and perversely I enjoy having to toughen up now and again
− Growth, personal development, confidence, competence, skill enhancement, self-awareness, and self-understanding
− Fun, enjoyment, laughs, and good times - it's not all about blisters, bogs and resilience

- Meeting people. All sorts of people
- Physical fitness, healthy lifestyle, lots of exercise and fresh air
- Having goals and achieving my vision

When people ask me how my Live Life to the Full mission started, I trace it back to my school days, and a minor rebellion involving a pair of red stilettos and a girl called Sherilee.

Until I was 13 I was a goody two-shoes. In fact my two "goody" shoes were dutifully polished, conker-brown, sensible Clarke's shoes with laces. At my secondary comprehensive school there was a girl called Sherilee, who was not like me at all. She was cool and I was square. She was rebellious; I conformed. She was often in trouble while I was in the teacher's good books. On July 14, we shared a birthday, and that day a gang at school bombed us with the traditional eggs and flour which resulted in us trying to un-glue our hair and pick out the eggshell in the girl's loos before our Chemistry lesson.

We bonded immediately and became friends, an unusual pairing which surprised both of us I think, and I began to borrow some leaves from her book of life. From then on I became more rebellious. I smoked and skived. I was in detention on my first day at Upper School for going into town at lunchtime without an exeat. I walked five miles home when I was bored or to skip lessons. I flirted with the boys in Maths. I worked at a garden centre on weekdays until one of the teachers rang up to ask why I wasn't in my English Literature lesson...

And I loved it. Because what this meant to me was that instead of being just another of the 1600 pupils keeping my head down and toeing the line as a middle class, Sussex schoolgirl was expected to do, I enjoyed myself and embraced the mess. I had lots of fun, adrenaline rushes, became notorious and popular, got street smart, strengthened my vivacity and spirit and stretched my personality; it was character building stuff. I don't regret it at all because it expanded my world, kick-starting my life into being bigger and better than perhaps it would have been.

Remarkably it was that very large comprehensive school that gave me my first alluring whiff of unpackaged adventure. Nine of us, seven students and two teachers, went to India for a month when I was 16. This was not your typical school trip to the Natural History Museum, eating cheese and onion crisps while staring at woolly mammoths. This was more about trying to eat spicy dal at 0530 while shooing an elephant off your washing. On this, my earliest expedition, I got my first taste of leaving the beaten track, staying in villages where they hadn't seen Westerners before and sleeping in tents among roaming tigers. I remember a pow-wow with the locals about whether it was entirely safe to have seven school children camping within range of the wild carnivores - I don't think health and safety would approve such a school trip these days!

It was risky, not always controlled or safe, but overwhelmingly an experience for us all. Memories I have decades later include playing cricket against the locals on a scorched, blood-red field, trying not to thwack the holy cows with the ball; going to sleep in the middle of a hut so the rats didn't run over our faces; receiving a dirty injection from an old rheumy-eyed Indian to reduce swelling from all my mosquito bites, and spraying "Impulse" deodorant spray into the long-drop toilets to mask the stench. While we were out there, and rather incredibly, we built a community centre for a remote village, constructed a wall out of mud and stones, and renovated an old well. It was an eye-opening, bottom-clenching, bone-shaking trip, full of discomfort and difficulty, but its very exotic and quixotic nature lured me into travelling a little bit more.

When I was 22, I took a year out and backpacked around-the-world, cramming in many fresh and strange experiences. According to my diary, I lived life to the full that year:

We travelled to seven countries and stayed in 79 different places, sleeping in a longhouse, a Dayak Chief's house, on a cargo boat, on a beach, in a hammock, in a traditional [Sumatran] Minangkabau house, in hill tribe huts, hotels, Losmen, youth hostels, home stays, guest houses, buses and houseboats.

We have seen the Taj Mahal, Mount Bromo, Dieng Plateau, Cameron Highlands, Kashmir, Kathmandu, Chitwan National Park, Bangkok's 'night life', Sydney Opera House and Harbour Bridge, Grand Prix, Great Barrier Reef, Borobudur, Prambanan, Bali, komodo dragons, a giant leatherback turtle laying her eggs, manta ray and turtle while scuba diving, Dayak longhouses, medicine men, a chief's funeral, ritual killing of buffalo, buffalos fighting, one-horned white rhino, Singapore, wave rock, canyons, flying foxes.

We have travelled on the back of an elephant, on top of a market truck while my friend was driving, in a becak, rickshaw, tuk-tuk, bemo, on a bicycle, a bamboo raft and motorbikes, various vessels – huge Pelni liners, motor launch, canoe, outrigger, river taxis, ces, longboats, '007' Bangkok boats, cargo boat, dinghy...

I have eaten frogs' legs, whole fish including the head and tail, rambutan, durian and jack fruit (and tonnes of rice!), and have drunk coconut, avocado, banana, pineapple, orange and papaya juice, Anggur Kuat, Chinese rum, moonshine, palm wine, rice wine, Hennessy cognac, jasmine tea, Chinese herbal tea, green tea and many kopi susu!

At the end of my diary, I concluded that:

For the good of my soul I have learned to be patient, adapt, cooperate, compromise, laugh at difficulties, smile when frustrated, be kind when feeling murderous, give situations / people the benefit of the doubt, try not to judge on first impressions and basically enjoy life – letting time flow without pressure and deadlines.

These varied, rewarding and rich experiences help me to fully live. And to fully live we must live life to the full; filling our lives with events, moments and memories to savour. But this is not just about doing, but being and becoming, for what grows inside us is greater than our activities and our belongings. We collect events and memories, and from them we build wisdom. Life is an adventure, a bracing, ambiguous journey, a quest to explore and discover and every memento contributes to the rich tapestry of life.

In the early days, at the end of each calendar year, I used to write down all the events and headlines for the past 12 months – such as going to India, passing my driving test or buying my first car (an orange MGB Roadster). After a few years of doing this I realised that some years were rather barren, while others were clearly eventful, so I decided to be more active in filling my time with interesting, stretchy, challenging, educational, rewarding, memorable, stimulating, satisfying, and soulful experiences. I started to plan my life pro-actively, beginning with the end in mind, working out what my vision was for living life to the full and how to make it happen.

My main strategy for achieving this is by having a list of aspirational goals – a list of all the things I want to do before I die. This is often called a "Bucket List" because it's what you want to do before you kick the bucket. I prefer to call it "Living Life to the Full" as this focuses on being alive rather than worrying about being dead! I don't limit myself to a list of "100 things to do before I die" because I want to keep living life to the full up until I die.

I have done over 115 things so far and my "done" list grows all the time as I tick things off, from small events to massive expeditions; from the mundane to the bizarre. They help me feel alive and know that when I am drawing my last breath, it will be with no regrets. I want to "fill the unforgiving minute with sixty seconds' worth of distance run." I want to cram my lifetime with 100 years of living life to the full with 36,500 days that were well worth it.

I have two lists – things I have done and things I want to do – and they contain a great diversity. My principle is that anything goes – it's my list and I can put on it what I like. It can be small, free or easy (like wild swimming), or huge and seemingly impossible (skiing the full distance to the South Pole). It can be crazy, physical, emotional, charitable, challenging or purely enjoyable. I have kayaked the length of the Thames from source to sea, walked on hot coals, sailed around the world, paddled the Mekong, trekked in West Papua, slept in gers with Mongolians, walked across England, climbed sand dunes in the Gobi desert, journeyed on the Trans-Siberian railway, ridden an ostrich, swam with dolphins, dived with great white sharks, written four books, got two degrees, skied to the South Pole, attempted stand up paddle boarding, husky sledding and caving, taken part in La Tomatina and the world bog snorkelling championships, ran a marathon, cycled from London to Brighton ten times in fancy dress, delivered a TED talk...

Currently I have on my "To Do" list: sleep at the ice hotel, take part in the World Worm Charming Championships, learn to whistle through my fingers, go to Alaska, trek across a desert, have tea at Buckingham Palace and write this book.

I add to my "To Do" list constantly, always open to inspiration. The more people I talk to, the more inspirational suggestions I get. I frequently ask, "What do you want to do before you die?," "Where have you been that's amazing?," "What do you think I should do next?," and people love having conversations about this. I once did a talk at a retirement home and unashamedly stole one lady's ambition - to live to be 100. That's now on the list. We spark off each other, and suggestions I like go straight onto my phone and then onto my website. If it's written down, I am more likely to do it, which is one of my tips for accomplishing a Live Life List. Here are my Top Ten:

1) Take time out to list all the things you have done already. You will have done more than you think. Celebrate and be proud of these.

2) Then brainstorm all the things you want to do and places you want to visit. You can go online, ask friends, read travel magazines and Things to Do Before You Die books, and gradually that list will build. Remember this is your list; full

of stuff YOU want to do. It doesn't have to stack up or compare to anyone else's.

3) Once you have your list, record it - write it onto a whiteboard, create a charter, put it on your website, an App, stick it to a bucket – because the more real it is, the more it solidifies, the more likely you are to do it.

4) Every now and again review the list and depending on how much time and money you have at that point, choose one to do next. Just one. Make them happen one at a time.

5) Take a big positive step to start: book the tickets, sign the contract, enter the competition, buy the boat...

6) **Give yourself positive beliefs and positive labels**. Stay positive. Stay constructive. No excuses. No buts. No, I can't... Because then you are limiting your beliefs which will affect your confidence and whether you go for it or not.

7) **Choose your attitude**. You can choose to be fearful and worried and limited and unable, or you can choose to challenge yourself, step up and stretch, embrace the fear and embrace the mess. The more you stretch, the more alive you will feel.

8) Give it **100% commitment**. No half-hearted efforts. If you're going to do something, do it to the best of your ability with your whole heart, body, mind and soul. Raise your game.

9) Update both your lists. We all like ticking things off lists, so once you have done something, take it off your "To Do" and put it on your "Done."

10) Celebrate. Breathe. Savour.

This book is about some of my adventures and lessons I have learned along the way. I want you to find inspiration in it – not only that, but the determined *will* to do something you really want to do in your life. The hardest part is taking the first step. I meet so many people who say to me, "I wish I could do that" or

"I've always wanted to do that." My reply, "Go on then." **If the will is there, then there is a way**.

I have included some of the principles above - and more - in a list at the back of this book, which should help you. You only live once so embrace it, ride it, fill it, use it, spend it, and make the most of it.

Embrace the Mess and **Lean In**.

Chapter 2
Just Do It!

One day I quit my job in London; five months later I was racing around Cape Horn on a 67' yacht, heeled over, riding 22 metre waves at 0400 in freezing conditions and missing three crew after two medical evacuations. Clearly my life had taken a dramatic change of direction. I had made a handbrake turn at the crossroads and chosen a chancy route signposted "Just Do It," which pointed towards an uncertain, precarious and exciting future.

It started with a blind date in my local pub in Clapham, South West London. I'd arranged to meet a gentleman and I spotted him as soon as I walked in the door. He was wearing a woolly scarf and a flat cap and looked a fair bit older than his photograph. I realised it wasn't going to be love at first sight, but I enjoy meeting new people and I joined him for a friendly chat with the notion of romance far from my thoughts.

We shared stories and whilst talking about my current work situation, I explained that I had a serious case of itchy feet. I was feeling restless. Everything was fine; my life was good, but I felt too comfortable and I needed a challenge. He mentioned a poster he had noticed that day on the London Underground about an amateur-crewed, round-the-world yacht race. It got me thinking. I felt a flicker of excitement, a stirring of my spirit, a spark had been ignited… and as I sat in that warm, dry pub on a winter's evening, with a perfectly nice man, drinking my Jack Daniels and Coke, I wondered if this might be the answer.

The trouble was, I didn't know how to sail.

The Global Challenge was called "The World's Toughest Yacht Race" because it sails the wrong way around the world, westwards around Cape Horn and twice into the Southern Ocean against the prevailing waves and winds. If you can imagine sailing with the wind behind you, the spinnaker sail up, surfing the waves with a gin and tonic in your hand… well, it's not like that. Sailing westwards, the boat is constantly bashing against the waves and beating into the wind, so it's a lot tougher, a lot bouncier and a lot slower. It's also one of the world's most endurance-based sporting competitions in that it lasts ten months from start to finish, 24-hours a day.

When I competed as a core crew member, the race involved 12 boats. Each boat had a professional, paid skipper and 17 amateur crew who paid for their places. I applied in May; my place was confirmed with Team Stelmar on the 19th of July and we set sail on the 3rd of October, so I had just over two months to prepare, train, get my life in order – and learn to sail. That focuses the mind.

It is fair to say that I was quite lost and anxious initially and I had plenty of reasons – or shall we call them excuses – stacking up, whispering in my head to give up and do something cheaper, easier and kinder. What was I doing putting myself through so much anxiety? Was it nuts or guts?! Here is my list of "I can't do this because…"

- I have a full time job that I love and I am very lucky to have it
- I am a shareholder and I will have to sell my shares and quit the company
- It will damage my long term career
- I own a flat in London
- I can't afford £35,000 plus lose a year's salary

- I could do so much more with £35,000
- I need to save money for my pension / mortgage / cost of living
- I can't go away for a year!
- I can't sail
- I get seasick
- I'm not sure I will enjoy it / it sounds pretty scary
- My mum will kill me!

All are good enough reasons not to do something, but there was one big reason on the other side of the scales: Living Life to the Full, with the underlying principle: **Just do it**.

"Just do it"; three simple - but certainly not simplistic - words. Just do it. Make it happen. Take a leap; don't think about it too hard, don't weigh up the pros and cons, don't get tangled up in knots or held down by hundreds of inhibitive ties like Gulliver in the land of Lilliput...These seemingly innocuous words sound easy, an over-used slogan, a flippant remark, but the commitment is not. Underneath the surface is a not insignificant requirement for courage, effort and strength. Ellen MacArthur - female yacht racing legend - spent a lot of time in France and adopted the phrase "à donf," which essentially means go for it. I also believe in à donf. "Maybe, possibly, perhaps" doesn't get you anywhere. Just do it, go for it or à donf in any language takes you on at least an interesting journey, plus hopefully somewhere worthwhile. **No regrets.**

For those who need a more definite answer, a more complete argument, here is my positive, commitment list of "I WILL do this because:"

- It will be a fantastic once-in-a-lifetime experience full of excitement, adventure, thrills and challenges
- It will stretch and develop me
- It will be about Living Life to the Full
- It means no regrets
- It will add a significantly interesting chapter to my life
- It will enhance my career in the long term

- It may be scary and difficult but that's OK
- I may not enjoy all of it, but that's OK
- I can surmount most other obstacles
- I CAN leave my job and sell my shares
- I CAN make the finances work
- I CAN rent out my flat
- I CAN learn to sail
- I CAN survive seasickness
- My Mum won't kill me
- I CAN make my Mum proud of my achievements, etc.

There is only ever one thing stopping you from achieving your goals, and that one thing is yourself; if you are determined enough to succeed, then you will. **If the will is there, then there is a way**.

To be fair, I did have a little sailing experience. I had been out on my uncle's boat – a 32' Moody – about three times when I was twelve years old out of Poole Harbour. As far as I recall, the experience wasn't always positive and is probably what stopped me from taking up sailing. I have miserable recollections of feeling sick and being cold. I don't think I had much idea about what was going on or where we were; I just had the usual "Mind out for the boom!" drummed in, which rather scared me.

Twenty-five years later I felt the same about sailing. I still clung to the memories of sickness, cold and uncertainty. Yet here I was, signed up for the Global Challenge, something most applicants had yearned for since they were children as they planned, saved and applied to join the race five years in advance of the start. I had never heard of the race before May. With my place only confirmed in mid-July, I had two months to learn to sail before we left on 3 October.

I couldn't just drop everything to learn to sail, however. Having quit my job, I was also working out my notice - full time - for the much needed funds. The trip itself would cost £35,000 and I wouldn't be earning for a year. I had two months to pull together the money, take part in training and qualifying sails every other week, go to the gym six days a week, attend team meetings, weekly conference calls and carry out other team responsibilities, sort my life out for being away for a year and learn to sail. I'd been sent wads of Global Challenge forms, manuals and paperwork and one of my many tasks was to learn it all. Here is one paragraph from my 160-page training manual:

> Before **tacking** or **gybing**, *make sure that both the* **traveller lines** *are secure...also remember that after the* **tack** *or* **gybe***, the* **windward** *and* **leeward** *sides will have swapped! The* **Cunningham** *is employed by attaching the* **Cunningham** *line to the* **cringle** *just above the* **tack***, and then applying tension. The* **flattener eye** *is positioned just above the* **clew** *of the sail... the* **leech line***...*

I laughed. It made no sense to me whatsoever; I was in at the deep end. It is hard enough to learn a new sport or discipline but the language that comes with sailing makes it more inaccessible to the novice. I had no idea what a cringle or a Cunningham was, they just sounded like funny words. I also discovered a "barber hauler" during the race which was another name for "some rope." I was confused around the word tack – because you can tack a boat and the forward corner of the sail is called a tack; the terminology really didn't help me feel at ease with learning to sail. It was an alien world and I was out of my comfort zone by a few nautical miles.

By the start day I was not ready. But then often in life we aren't ready, or will never be 100% ready, and we just have to give it our best shot, be positive, embrace the nerves and *just do it*. Spending too much time teetering on the edge, waiting for that perfect moment, perfect knowledge or perfect ability is unrealistic; sometimes that moment never comes; often waiting means losing momentum or nerve.

I had far from perfect knowledge or ability when I started the Global Challenge. I spent as much time as I could training and becoming familiar with sailing before I left, but I was still a greenhorn. I attended three training sails and swotted up on dry land with dry books as much as possible in between working, getting fit, renting my flat out, arranging visas, team building, raising funds and all that goes with such a monumental challenge. I found my days getting longer and longer as I woke earlier and earlier to fit in the administration and learning, and went to bed later and later after fitness classes and goodbye drinks with friends. My time awake and being active ran to 18 hour days in the last month before I left and I was exhausted by the start of the race. It was not at all easy joining this way - with so much less experience than the 17 others on my boat - but more rewarding in that I had such a huge chasm to bridge between my starting weight and finishing weight. I had to stretch more than the others but that also meant that I learnt more and grew more.

I was not a sailor by any stretch of the imagination. I still did not know all the lingo, I couldn't navigate, helm or trim very well, I had great difficulty moving around above and below decks and I felt like a burden on my high performing racing team. I was worried that I'd mess up, potentially ruin our performance or, worst case, physically hurt myself or someone else with my ineptitude. The boats were 22-metre, steel-hulled, 40-tonne vessels; they were very manual and heavy racing yachts with powerful forces at play. Not the most tolerant of training grounds.

This lack of competence - and confidence - could have been a disaster, preventing me from being willing to give things a go. I would have been in my panic zone, concentrating on survival, in my own shut-off, frightened and uncomfortable world. But I didn't let that happen. I screwed up my courage and set off, unready and ill-prepared, physically sick and feeling cold (like when I was a child) in a force eight gale. It was a horrendous start to a ten-month race. We had a "Man Overboard" within 12 hours of the start! But I did it. I did the best I could and got through the first few days, step by step, hour by hour, and watch by watch.

After the first week, my sickness subsided and I was able to eat and move about the boat without banging or bruising my body. I could do most of my jobs without someone helping me. And I began to enjoy it.

We are, I believe, more capable than we realise.

The more we live in our comfort zone, and not step into the stretch zone, the less we will learn, the less capable and skilled and wise and experienced we will become, and the more stuck we will find ourselves in our safe, controlled place.

However, we are capable. We CAN do. And the more we believe we can, the more we will do. If we think we can, we can; if we think we can't, we won't. We have positive and negative beliefs about ourselves, and the negative beliefs or labels will limit us and the positive ones will set us free. Which is why "just do it" can sometimes be the answer, because if we take the leap, the leap liberates us from our limits. Leaping takes courage, *just doing it* takes courage, and the big stuff needs courage, otherwise it wouldn't be big. Teetering on the edge, or taking small steps, doesn't get you across the chasm between where you are now and where you want to be.

People can limit themselves (and therefore the breadth and depth of their lives) with negative labels or negative beliefs. We can step out and away from those constrictions to give something a go and get started. I couldn't sail before I took on the Global Challenge, which could have been a limiting belief, or I could give it my best shot and no-one could have a problem with that.

If I had clung to my negative beliefs that I couldn't sail, that I was a burden to my team, that I really shouldn't be taking part in such a long and competitive yacht race, then I wouldn't have gone for it; I wouldn't have applied or I wouldn't have stuck it out. I would have either not entered, believing it was way out of my realm, or I would have quit at some point as the negative doubts took over my head. However, I *believed* that I could learn, and that I had the right attitude to become a valuable member of the team and I think **attitude is 95% of the game**.

My attitude towards the race was pragmatic (I needed to learn and get on with it as fast as I could) but aspirational; I had an innate strength of character and determination that would set me in good stead. I set my mind to being positive and constructive, very much in the spirit of "this girl can." I call this *feasible belief*. I had to have belief to fill the gap between what was being asked of me and what I actually thought I was able to do, but the belief was grounded in the knowledge that if I applied myself, persevered, stayed focused, was open to learning and tried hard, then I was in with a fighting chance.

I took the leap, tried very, very hard and found myself on a 67' yacht racing around Cape Horn, as I said, heeled over, riding 22 metre waves at 0400, in freezing conditions and missing three crew after two medical evacuations. Cape Horn is to the sailor as Everest is to the mountaineer. The Southern Ocean behaves as if the Himalayas have come to life in a dynamic, fluid force of nature, where mountainous waves heave and roll in giant peaks and valleys that are freezing, turbulent and treacherous. At the bottom of a trough between two Southern Ocean waves, translucent green walls of water loom on either side, darkening the air.

The Southern Ocean, also known as the Antarctic Ocean, is actually a combination of seas, straits and gulfs below 60 degrees South that circumnavigates Antarctica in a continuous churning cycle. Cape Horn is both the narrowest and shallowest part that the great mass of water has to funnel through, so the seas pile up, the waves grow bigger and there is more agitation and disturbance. Not only is the ocean in its most dangerous state there, but the weather is almost continually stormy. Gales and storms chase each other in quick succession around the Southern diameter of the globe. Cycles of snow, sleet and hail constantly pass through. Boats become tiny, insignificant dots, violently pitching and tossing, with frozen sails and ropes, freezing waves crashing over the foredeck and snow-laden rigging and lines.

Our steel-hulled, 67' boat is like a fragile toy, a plaything to the capriciousness of the powerful and commanding ocean. The boat doggedly climbs up a steep cliff-face, where, for a moment, she hangs suspended and exposed in the thick of the spray and the sleet beneath the dark, ominous clouds and wheeling albatross. She perches, momentarily on the brink, before crashing down the other side, down, down...18, 20, 22 metres. The whole boat judders. The rigging shakes. A great volume of water crashes along the deck picking up crew and carrying them along the boat towards the stern, as they grab winches and rails to stop their flight. There is a Force 11 storm and snow is in the air. The mainsail is lashed down to the mast. 60 mile per hour winds screech off the ice-sheet of Antarctica. I am on deck, freezing cold, hanging on for dear life... and loving it. I am on a long and extreme fairground ride.

I didn't love it at first. I was too panicky, cold and uncomfortable to remotely enjoy it. I was in survival mode for the first week or so.

When we left Buenos Aires for the second leg of the Global Challenge round-the-world yacht race, half the crew were excited about going round Cape Horn and into the Southern Ocean, and half were fearful. I was one of the latter. I was itching to get back out there, yet anxious about what was to come. This leg of the race was going to be the toughest in the world's toughest yacht race. Out of Buenos Aires along the river Plate, then turning south along the dramatic coastline of Tierra del Fuego, around Cape Horn and westwards into the Southern Ocean. Then we would sail in freezing, desolate and stormy conditions for a whole month to Wellington, New Zealand. The leg overall was due to take about 40 days, covering 6100 nautical miles.

A few days into the leg, as we sailed alongside Tierra del Fuego the coastline was stunning and captivated me whenever I drew breath to take a savouring look at the passing scenery. But as we voyaged south, the weather worsened, the waves got bigger and the cold began to sting. As conditions deteriorated, I clung on with white knuckles, freezing and miserable, scared for my life and not at all enjoying the ride.

The storms were relentless – all day and every day was akin to battling a gale in mid-winter – which eventually became the norm. As we headed south on the boat, day by day, watch by watch, I began to adapt. What I had thought was rough weather and stormy seas before - like crossing the Bay of Biscay at the start of the race in October - was comparatively benign. The Southern Ocean was so much more volatile in comparison and I learned to deal with it. We are amazingly adaptive creatures. We learn to reconfigure our perceptions and recalibrate our "this is tough/dangerous/scary" yardsticks. We rescale our thinking relative to our experiences.

I progressively learned to let go, mentally and physically, within the extreme conditions. I worked through my fear and in time comprehended that the boat was designed to behave like a cork – to stay bobbing on top of those giant waves. My mind was finally relaxed enough to become cognisant of boat physics – the Archimedes principle, that although the boat was tossed about like a toy, it had a buoyant force. I had been fixed on the fear that the boat – our only sanctuary in this most inhospitable environment – was going to capsize or pitch-pole, and we would all die, but logically it was designed not to and I developed a rationale over my feelings. I adjusted my beliefs and changed my attitude, embracing the magnificence of our environment rather than fighting against its malevolence.

This more accepting attitude also relaxed me physically. I learned how to move with the boat, bending my knees in anticipation of crashing downwards, and grabbing a handhold in anticipation of the boat launching upwards. One day, sitting in our "Zero-G lounge" in the forepeak where our sails heaved and breathed as the boat roller-coastered up and down, I realised I was laughing; things must be improving.

These days, if I go sailing in stormy weather, even though I have sailed the Southern Ocean and subsequently crewed for the RNLI, I still find it hard to acclimatise because there is no gentle gradient of adjustment. One moment you are on land, in a dry, secure and comfortable place, with buildings, shelter and warmth, and the next, launched off into a treacherous, dynamic environment. It takes a fresh "go for it" attitude from me every time.

* * *

Sailing around the world was a reasonably large undertaking which I took on without much hesitation. I knew in my heart and gut that it was going to be an amazing experience with a big purpose – to live life to the full. I had to go for it. To just do it and jump in with 100% commitment, even though I was not 100% ready or 100% perfect; sooner or later the day comes when you just have to start. If the end goal was the sole focus, far, far away, then most people wouldn't even take the first step. The end goal can drive and motivate people to be forward looking, but the next single step ensures action. Taking action, taking at least one step towards a goal or on a journey, is a positive start with positive energy.

Embarking on change or a challenge can be exciting, but difficult. Anthony Robbins, the American motivational guru, suggests that we commence with "massive and immediate action" to get going with stretchy goals, taking a big first step at the start. This stimulates momentum and energy because where the focus goes, the energy flows. The first step can be the hardest because the decision or the commitment behind that step requires the bigger leap. Hesitating or faltering at the start can freeze resolve with indecision, uncertainty or fear. Once the mental resolve is reached, then the physical movement should quickly follow before the commitment cools or inertia replaces momentum.

It's the same for the simple resolution to go to the gym or for a swim. A positive decision carries positive energy, which boosts the physical body to act, and together the heart, mind, body and spirit collaborate to carry you forwards. Last week I determined to go wild swimming in my local creek. This was a free and easy, live life to the full mini-adventure. The creek is just five minutes

Paula Reid

away and I was frustrated that I hadn't plucked up the energy to swim in it yet. It was mid-October and a bit chilly, but in theory the water would be enjoying post-summer temperatures and it was one of those tranquil, blue-sky autumnal days. Two swans were in the creek when I got there, looking serene and part of the scene, but slightly putting me off! There was also a council workman in a high-vis jacket nearby making me feel self-conscious too. If I had stood there contemplating it for too long, I may have gone home again. I had to just do it, swans, workman, cold creek and all, so I stripped down to my swimsuit, waded in and dove under the water.

Coming straight back up gasping for breath and muttering something unrepeatable about the cold, I was then committed and went for the most glorious, soul-fulfilling, peaceful swim to the bridge and back. The water was clear, trees reflected along one side, with blue sky overhead and swans keeping me company. 45 minutes later I waded back out with my spirit singing. It had been worth it, every step. The first step had been to commit to a wild swim in October, the second was to put on my swimsuit that morning, the third was to go to the creek and the fourth was to dive in. Each step needed my resolve and momentum because the lure of NOT doing it was strong, but I was pleased and proud to have done it and I felt much better for it. How else could I have got my "spirit singing" in October? Certainly not sitting at the laptop!

Sometimes starting, taking the first step, means doing so with no preparation, planning or practice. "Just do it" implies some impulsiveness and there are times when spontaneity is best. I do plan and prepare thoroughly for the big and dangerous expeditions, with a respect for the conditions and knowing that you can't beat having the best kit and the right knowledge. But there are other times when it is very liberating not to plan and train; to just run and jump in.

Spontaneity when it comes to travel is natural and emancipating; it carries the impetus, energy and excitement of leaping. There is no pressure to be ready. There are no expectations. Spontaneity brings a flexibility of agenda, a liberation of attitude, pleasant surprises, freedom, the permission to wander and the agility to make the most of opportunities as they arise. To just go and see where the path takes you.

Planning can be advisable; preparation can safeguard your experience. However, *not* planning can result in the discovery of a more natural and wonderful sight than in any guide book; no preparation can mean travelling "fast and light" and "going local" for the whole experience. I have had some of my more rewarding encounters thanks to no planning, no preparation and being spontaneous – just doing it. I really enjoy just taking off with a backpack and some money and delighting in the exploration and discovery experience. If I am going on a trek, or a backpacking adventure, or a fun event, I like to have a "head-torch" approach and just light up the way as I go, uncovering the secrets in my beam, with no expectations or assumptions. I trust the adventure or journey will reveal itself and I feel more fully present, open-minded and open-eyed when I travel this way.

Four of my most enjoyable expeditions were achieved spontaneously and on my own doorstep in the UK. These trips needed a little preparation, a tent and a backpack, and some money for sustenance on route, but that's about it. And for that minimal amount of investment, I got back a huge return in experiences, memories and photos. Each trip comprised hundreds of mini events and sights that patch-work together into a whole fantastic journey.

* * *

Kayaking the Thames was such a "just do it" trip. I undertook this with my other half, Alex, whom I had met on the Global Challenge. We had to pay for a lock licence, which wasn't much, a man with a van to drop us off and pick us up, and borrowed two touring kayaks from two different friends. Our main cost was the Thameside pub lunches and dinners we indulged in – with a few bottles of wine.

I had already paddled the Mekong River in Cambodia and the San Juan River in Nicaragua in dugout canoes and I had a hankering to paddle an English river - almost as a pilgrimage or a tribute to our own beautiful waterways. Not sure how far we would get or where we would start and finish, I did some research on the English Waterways and Thames Locks websites and asked for advice from colleagues, the RNLI and a couple of friends who had done some British kayaking. It turned out that there is a known route kayaking the Thames from "Source to Sea" - starting near the source of the Thames - Cricklade or Lechlade - and finishing at what is officially called the "sea" where it becomes tidal after Teddington Lock. Perfect! Beyond this point one would have to kayak through the city of London and the Thames Barrier onto the Tideway downstream towards Tilbury Docks, which required more kit and experience. We decided to do "source to sea" and get out at some point after Teddington Lock, depending on how long we had, perhaps leaving the remaining reaches of the Thames for another time. We arranged for a van to pick us and the kayaks up from my parents' place near Gatwick and drop us off at the source, with another (ice-cream) van picking us up at the finish.

We applied for a lock licence, stuck laminated names on our kayaks (Thames Tiger and Thames Tigress) and packed some dry bags. That was all the preparation we did. No kayaking experience, no training, no first aid kit or comms plan or specific arrangements around campsites or distances. We had "dry-sat" in the kayaks in my parents' garden to adjust the foot straps, but that was it. With a fairly spontaneous decision to kayak the Thames, we then "just did it." The van driver, Stan, dropped us off at Cricklade where there was a trickle of a stream that was the start of the Thames and knowing that we hadn't kayaked before, looked at us as if we were mad. Clearly struggling with his conscience before he dumped us and drove away, he asked incredulously: "Are you sure? This is it? You know what you're doing and you're OK from here?"

We happily and confidently assured him we were fine and excited to start. Within half an hour I had fully tipped over and was submerged, with several items including my iPhone at the bottom of the Thames. Luckily I managed to grope around in the mud and find all my kit as the river was so shallow at this point. I also found an underwater branch which I blamed for the reason I had tipped in. Alex had laughed at me but fell in two hours later trying to get into the kayak after a pub lunch. It wasn't the booze, honest – it just took a bit of adjustment for us to find our balance! This lack of finesse was one of the downsides of not training and prepping thoroughly, but we had momentum, energy and laughter on our side.

That afternoon we were wet and cold after both of our unexpected dunkings and feeling a little bit forlorn. We knew we had to camp somewhere that night but probably without facilities and would have to pitch our tent while we were damp and chilly. This is a typical whining moment for me where I am more fractious and unhappy than when I am really up against it fighting for survival. Kayaking along in water about a metre deep that was freely flowing, I was mumbling and grumbling about being cold and not enjoying it so much at that moment. I was in the lead kayak and Alex was paddling desultorily behind me, both wrapped up in our own damp, cold worlds, trying to motivate ourselves with the thought of warm fires and a pub dinner – lasagne or pie and mash perhaps. As I advanced round a bend in the river, I saw paddling towards us a bunch of lads in an eclectic mix of canoes and kayaks towing a rubber dingy full of booze! They cheerfully called out to me, laughing and shouting and rather flirting - until Alex appeared around the bend - and invited us to join them on the river bank for an impromptu party. Thirty minutes later I was warming nicely by a crackling fire on the river bank, drinking a glass of full-bodied red and chatting to some lovely guys whom it turned out were mates of my friend Mark who had lent me my kayak. Small and delightful world! This perked us up no end and Alex and I set off again with renewed vigour - and a slight tipsiness which helpfully made our paddling more decisive and robust. All was right with the world again.

We had fabulous times as we kayaked along the Thames among the swans, Henley Regatta, the Fairford air show and the fine pubs strung along the riverside. Each night we camped on the river bank - occasionally in official campsites, but preferably in pub gardens (with permission) or wild camping on public tracts of land. One evening we pulled up and found a lovely stretch of luxuriant, high quality grass (nice and spongy to sleep on), near a wood and a decent pub. Brilliant! We pitched up and strolled to the pub for a well-earned dinner and bottle of red before retiring for the night.

At 0500 the next morning we were crudely awakened by a huge and angry security guard shouting at us to get out of the tent IMMEDIATELY as he shone his torch at us, took photos and demanded our names and addresses. It turned out that we had in fact mistaken the public bit of land nearby with the adjoining estate belonging to a very wealthy but reclusive millionaire. The security guard had just come on watch and was understandably horrified that his highly expensive, 24-hour security system had been foiled by a couple of easy-going, low-tech campers. On the positive side, I saw it as a free test of his security system and wondered about selling our services as "security testers" where we would try and camp in as many posh gardens and private estates as possible for a small fee...

After a fiery ten minutes or so, during which time we felt comprehensively interrogated and intimidated, we all managed to calm down, smile and shake hands. The guard recognised that we had made an innocent mistake and apologised for his severity, even offering to make us a cup of tea before we set off. It was still only 0530 but he did insist that we leave the premises, quite understandably, so we had an unusually early start to our kayaking that day. But often with adversity comes opportunity and some kismet somewhere redresses the balance and gives back. We packed our tent, smiling wryly at the memory of our traumatic start to the morning and the transformation of the guard from interrogator to teaboy (tea being fairly critical to the start of a good day for me, wherever I am) and then, as we turned towards our kayaks to start loading, there was a sight to catch the breath.

The sun was rising over the Thames and shining weakly through the low-lying morning mist. Swans were leisurely waking up and preening themselves on the green lawns sloping down the river bank, making gentle honking noises as they groomed and smoothed feathers through their beaks, and a rainbow-coloured hot air balloon was rising just in front of us, puffing and blowing, next to the pale buttery ball of sun.

Paula Reid

Chapter 3
One Step at a Time

The 192-mile Wainwright's Walk from St Bees Head in Cumbria to Robin Hood's Bay in North Yorkshire, known as the Coast-to-Coast walk, connects three National Parks from one side of England to the other. The Lake District is the first if you go from West to East. This beautiful and impressive scenery then turns flat and agricultural as the trail leads you through the North York Dales, before changing once more into the stunning, heather-clad North York Moors. The whole route is varied, in a parade of hills, dales, lakes, fields, farms, footpaths, moors and cliffs; this was a rich and rewarding experience complete with furious, drenching, crazy rain, campsites on farms where lambs trot alongside hoping for a feed, and miles of purple heather and cackling grouse on the moors.

When Alex and I chose to do the Coast-to-Coast we were hardly prepared. We hadn't completed a multi-day walk before, we hadn't walked in our new boots and we had bought our tent on special offer in that famous outdoor shop - Halfords! The night before we set out, I looked up "preparation" on the C2C website and under training it said: "Probably the minimum that would get you by is two 15-mile walks back to back." The last time we'd done a walk was for five miles, two months before.

We were more than a little unprepared and apprehensive, but knew that it was a question of "one step at a time" and that everything starts with the first step. Just do it! Here is an excerpt from my diary on the first day, six hours before we started:

> *Well, here we are in Euston Station about to set off on our epic adventure. We've worked out that we're not allowed to camp where we're going, we're not allowed to start fires, we're not quite sure what the route is or how many miles we will be able to do each day, we've only got 12 days to do it, we haven't tried our tent out. Hey ho, we'll see how we get on. **I'm determined to do it**.*

As I was writing my diary on the tube, a guy accidentally stood on my foot and apologised.

"Don't worry," he said, "you have another one."

"No, I need them both because I'm off to do a 190 mile walk."

On Day One we did 8½ miles from St Bees Head to Cleator; we were crippled by the end of it and went to a pub. Crippled, crippled, crippled and I thought we'd never be able to walk another step. From getting off the train at St Bees, we had started walking at 1430 so weren't expecting a big mileage day, and we set off in great spirits, enjoying the view from the headland before turning eastwards to nip away at the miles towards the other coast, one step at a time. It was a clear day in August, not too hot, and we had plenty of energy bubbling away inside us; we'd framed this day as an easy day to get us started.

For the first few miles we chatted and joked and enjoyed the scenery, then we got quieter, and a little lost at one point which forced us to do extra miles - which made us even quieter, and then we started slogging. I know 8½ miles doesn't sound much, especially in light of the average 18 miles a day we were achieving once we got going, but I don't think we were physically or mentally ready for just a "walk" to be challenging. We thought a walk was just a walk and had underestimated the grit that it takes for repeated long-distance days carrying rucksacks. Alex didn't even have walking poles. Our new boots hadn't been worn in – classic beginner's error – and mentally we were struggling with the concept that just walking was quite hard after the first 90 minutes of fresh energy and stimulating scenery.

Part of the problem – apart from the lack of preparation and training – was that we had chosen to carry our own backpacks whereas most people who do this route have Sherpa vans transporting their stuff from point to point. So our main source of pain was our knees – the discomfort of walking 18+ miles each day with the weight of our backpacks bearing down whilst having to climb over all those lovely English stiles! There were days when we must have clambered up and over 30 stiles, as well as tackling the rolling ups and downs of the Lake District.

On that first evening we found a farmer's field to camp in – with the permission of the very chatty and friendly farmer – and once the tent was up to the wary fascination of the Friesians, we collapsed and had the joy of pulling obdurate boots and steaming socks off our throbbing feet. We were so done in that after a brief respite we even debated whether the energy was there to walk about a mile to the local pub for dinner. Agreeing that it was more appealing on balance than sitting hunched over in a 1.5-person tent for the whole evening, we reluctantly pulled our boots on again and hobbled up to the pub, laughing at our crippled gait. It was the right decision. The evening walk did us good and our legs eased a little from the stiffness that had started to set in.

On Day Two we started off feeling OK, after popping a couple of painkillers, a banana and some sports energy tablets. There was a 252-metre uphill schlep in the first half hour up Dent Fell and then down again to Ennerdale Bridge and a pub lunch. I am not a fan of trekking up hills or mountains, but I woke up mentally prepared to take Dent one step at a time, and that is how I attacked all the Lake District's ascents. Always happy striding down, I struggle on the ups, sometimes having to walk diagonally, progressing upwards in a shallow zig-zag pattern.

Provided that I keep moving, I know that every step is a step closer to the top and that I will eventually get there to enjoy the views over the other side. At the top of Dent the reward was indeed worth slogging up there for, with views across the Cumbrian coast and the Isle of Man. It was at this first inland high point on our walk when I looked to the West and the sea, and then towards the East in the direction we were heading, that our mission truly struck me. We had talked about the "coast to coast," but now we were literally walking the walk from one side of England all the way to the other. We would journey the whole width of the country solely using leg power. This realisation inspired me for the rest of the trip.

Sometimes step by step means surviving in the short term; sometimes step by step means scratching away at the far-off destination or whopping great goal. These first days were both. We were in survival mode - "let's just get up this hill first" - and eating away at the 192 miles between where we were and where we wanted to be. The remaining amount of country we had to walk over seemed daunting, but we were inspired and driven by the end goal and by the thought that every step was progress. We were on a journey as well as a quest to reach a destination.

In the valley following Dent, we walked around Ennerdale Water, which was beautiful, but Alex's legs started to hurt about two-thirds of the way so we were slightly crippled again by the end of the day. We stayed at "Black Sail Hut Youth Hostel" and slept in our tent amongst the slugs, foxes and midges. And it rained, rained, rained, rained, rained, rained, and rained. As Day Three started, wet and cloudy, there were midges everywhere, my eyes were swollen with tiredness and damp and I was getting offended by the slug invasion! There were slugs everywhere – shiny, moist black ones and fat, corrugated brown ones; all over the tent, our food bags and inside our boots.

But I had written in my diary: "I am determined to do it." In Euston Station I had mentally resolved to see this one through and if that meant one step at a time, then that was how we would complete it. So despite having very tempting conversations about walking to the nearest travel agent and booking a week in the sun, we persevered through the pain step by step, and both confess now that it was one of the best experiences we have had.

Once past the first two days of "acclimatisation," we felt more physically comfortable and mentally in the zone. Day Three was great and we over-achieved our mileage, making up for the slower start and putting some extra miles in the bag. By late afternoon we had reached our destination according to Wainwright's route which was Rosthwaite in Borrowdale, and amazingly still had energy left to do some more. We knew that if we pushed on, we were unlikely to reach civilisation in the daylight, but we fancied the psychological advantage of beating the set mileage of the route and the personal satisfaction of counter-balancing our earlier ineptitude. It's strange how the mind works.

Alex and I met doing the Global Challenge so it's hardly surprising that we have a relationship based on deep understanding and a very synergistic approach to living life to the full. We both had the physical stamina to push on and we both mentally wanted to put some extra miles in and "beat the system." We also quite fancied wild camping on the moors above Rosthwaite. So after buying some snacks for dinner / breakfast we pushed upwards, following a stream along Greenup Edge to Helm Crag ridge. I drank from the stream which was painfully, sparkling cold as we clambered upwards and got quite warm in doing so. On top, proud of our extra effort and extra mileage, we found a sweet spot to pitch our tent. Again, the exertion paid off, we were on our own, surrounded by stunning scenery, peaceful, inspired and loving it.

Over the next four days we walked through Patterdale, over Kidsty Pike - the highest point of the walk at 780 metres - and then sadly left the Lake District and crossed over the M6 in merciless rain to Keld. On Day Eight, we had a pleasant 12-mile walk from Keld to Gunnerside to Muker to Reeth, mostly following the banks of the River Swale on the Swale Way. Our good moods were further encouraged by the look of our campsite for the night – a delightful spot with caravans and tents pitched in an orchard. We had made good progress and arrived mid-afternoon. It was still warm and sunny so once we had pitched our tent, we got our camping mats out and lay in the sun, feet up on the rucksacks, reading our kindles. It was a blissful moment of restoration snatched indulgently from the daily toil. Just when we thought it couldn't get any better, the campsite owner arrived at our tent with a pot of tea, china mugs and home-made butterfly cakes on a tray! Two guys who had been dogging our footsteps the whole way arrived late afternoon and peering over the orchard wall caught us sipping our tea, little fingers bent, daintily nibbling at our cakes.

This walk was truly a perfect live life to the full experience and one that has impressed upon my memory among the more exotic, expensive and extreme adventures. I never thought that simply walking in my own country would give me so much pleasure. I had relegated it to when I was over 70 years old, with walking poles, a light rucksack containing sandwiches, a water bottle and a packet of polos; possibly with vehicle support carrying my bag and depositing it at hotels along the way. I was wrong. For all my chasing down of big expeditions, remote tribal trekking and white knuckle rides, I love going for long walks in Britain - it is "up there" in the best experiences - and it was really only *after* this first big walk that I realised how much I had enjoyed it. I had gained a fresh reverence for my own varied and fabulous country, the natural masterpieces of our countryside, our English weather and our brilliant national footpath network. Wainwrights' walk was like a pilgrimage to England's green and pleasant land. It was peaceful, beautiful and inspirational.

On Day 13, we walked up over the moors and the dramatic clifftop path along the Cleveland Way to arrive at the end of our journey - Robin Hood's Bay. The stunning view across the North Sea took our breath away as we realised anew that we had just walked across the whole country, one step at a time. The journey had been enriching and rewarding and we repeated the success of this first trek in later years by walking the Hadrian's Wall route from coast to coast, and then made up a trip from Dublin to Galway, from the East coast to the West coast of Ireland. Each time we set off with a feeble gait and a weak will we questioned why we had decided to put ourselves through it again. However, once on our way, we found our stride and marched to the beat of the drum, driven by the destination and inspired by the journey.

* * *

"One step at a time" is about achieving goals, dreams or destinations one chunk at a time; breaking down an ambition, journey or challenge into bite-size pieces, inch by inch, mile by mile, day by day. The very stretchy, or big, hairy and audacious goals (BHAG) can seem almost unachievable as we contemplate them from the starting line; standing far, far away from the distant and hazy end point. The expanse between where we stand and where we want to be can seem insurmountable or impossible; we may believe we are unable to go that far - physically or otherwise; that we fall short of the super-human criteria required for such a prodigious attempt. And so we stop ourselves from starting. We pull up at the first obstacle and put away that dream, or goal, or fail to strike out on that journey.

But if we break down giant ambition into manageable parts, then we feel able to achieve the first part; and once we start, we can go on to the second and third part, until we realise we are more capable than we think. We now have momentum on our side which brings energy and positivity. That first step, and then each step after that, is a commitment to moving forward and making progress. The big goals and the long journeys are achieved one step at a time if we keep scratching away at the mileage. Progress means evolution, development, advancement and growth. It's not just about the physical journey, the movement from A to B, it's also about our progress as individuals in our quest to live life to the full and realise our maximum potential.

On climbing Everest, Sir Edmund Hilary noted that his strong motivation helped him to "... *keep plugging on*" until ultimately, he set foot on the summit. Keep plugging on, or scratching away, or soldiering on, denotes dogged persistence, and dogged persistence needs a one step at a time approach. I use "one step at a time" as my mantra when I need to be in survival mode as it's equally applicable to relentless resilience and determination, especially against the odds. When the going gets tough, I put aside my end goal and concentrate on the here and now. I can't motivate myself any more with visualising the summit or final destination; they are too far away for me to think about during difficult times. In fact, the future end point can de-motivate me whilst I am grappling with the current crisis because it's an additional mental burden to carry. I can't divide my physical and psychological energy between surviving *and* beating a path to the top. I need to just survive, and only when I have got through the difficulty, can I then lift my head again and look to the finish. Survival Mode is very different to Everyday Expedition Mode. Survival Mode means putting the end point aside and concentrating on getting through the next hour, watch or leg, one step at a time.

Almost paradoxically then, there is the one step at a time mentality for achieving far off goals, and dissimilarly, the one step at a time approach for short-term survival. They both come into play, and have relevant strengths and benefits when played the right way round, during life-challenging, goal-stretching times. Both the journey and the destination are achievements and neither can be achieved in one stride.

* * *

Running the 26.3 miles of the London Marathon was also achieved one stride at a time. Here are my New Year's Resolutions from when I was 31:

- Give up smoking
- Lose weight
- Run the marathon
- Buy my flat

- Build career
- Look after myself
- Get a man
- Travel / adventure / rafting?

How Bridget Jones is that?!

This was going to be London Marathon year. On my very first training run, on Sunday 4th January, I felt righteous, superior and full of unrealised running potential in my fitness gear after the Christmas blowout. I set off and I pulled up after 300 yards. I was out of breath. OK, this was a surprise. I hadn't actually tried long distance running before and I'm not convinced my body is designed for it, but not to even manage a half mile! I was totally underwhelmed with myself. My first run, in full health, downhill, and I had failed. How was I going to keep up the training for the next four months, or run for five hours, when I couldn't even muster five minutes?

One step at a time.

I calculate that a marathon comprises about 50,000 steps...

I gritted my teeth. I rallied my resolve. The next day I put my trainers back on and went for my second run; it felt slightly better. The tops of my thighs ached from the day before and it poured with rain, but in spurts of effort I managed one whole mile, so that when I ran back, I felt like Jodie Foster in *Silence of the Lambs*. Hard core FBI agent in peak fitness: bring it on!

On the 10th of January I ran for two miles - hooray! I thought, I can do this. On Sunday, the 11th, just one week into my training, I ran five miles and although after the first half hour it was a struggle, I was proud. Here is my diary entry for Sunday, the 25th of January, three weeks into my training:

Partied and went to bed at 0430, then ran on Sunday morning. Dad drove me to Balcombe – as my plan is to do 'one way' running on the big runs – it gives me my incentive as there is no choice but to run home. The weather was foul, heavy rain and wind. So Dad dumped me in the middle of 'nowhere', 4½ miles from home, in my shorts, in the rain. I had to do my warm-up exercises and stretches at the side of the road but each time a car came I stopped and pretended to be walking along; self-conscious. Ran very well. Walked twice for about 15 paces each time, but apart from that I ran all the way home in 47 minutes. That was after another night of booze and no sleep – must be good for me! This means that every Saturday night I have to get drunk and go to sleep about 0400 in order to have a good run in the morning – Dave Bedford's style of running I think.

I worked on 10 minute miles, which is not particularly fast but then I'm not built for running, which means the 26.3 miles that would take Paula Radcliffe 2 hours 15 minutes would take Paula Reid 4 hours 25 minutes.

On the 15th of March I ran 12 miles and felt like Forrest Gump. I could run forever. I'd gone from Bridget Jones, to Jodie Foster, to Forrest Gump. Surely that meant my running prowess was improving? I trained and trained and trained until I was red in the face and felt sick, unable to eat after the long runs for a couple of hours. I was hardly ever in the "flow"; my running was usually a personal struggle involving discomfort, deep stitches and deeper effort.

The marathon itself was an acutely difficult day. At the start line in Blackheath I was nervous. It starts at 0930 and there were nine starting grids marked out for the masses (26,000 people). I had a throw-away sweatshirt on, Save the Rhino vest (I ran for Save the Rhino and Crohn's Disease), Lycra shorts, double-skin running socks, old Nike trainers, a Crohn's disease cap, Vaseline on my thighs and plasters on my nipples. A big cheer went up at the sound of the start cannon; we were off! But all that happened was that we swayed forwards, only to then walk the first mile and a half because there were so many people packed in.

I did nine minute miles for the first few hours and looked forward to seeing my friends and family half way by which time

(1200) it was absolutely tipping down, the streets were running rivers and the rain pecked into our eyes. I caught sight of Mum leaning out looking for me at Tower Bridge and with her were Dad and six friends – bless them all standing in the downpour to say hello and cheer me on. I trotted on the spot and happily chatted to them for a while then ran on, knowing that I wouldn't see anyone again until the end.

I felt absolutely fine at this point; I wasn't even consciously aware that I had been running, which was liberating. I was hoping naively that the euphoric atmosphere would carry me through to the end. However, at 16 miles I lost my energy, still with ten miles to go and those last two hours were killers. Many people were walking by now and at the pace I was running I was travelling at the same speed, so I thought I may as well walk too. Bad decision. As soon as I started walking my legs seized up and I had to stop to stretch all my muscles, then it was hugely painful to start running again. After that my ankle started to really hurt; then I had to stop and go to the toilet (you drink every mile and most of it gets sweated out but with the rain and cold, we all got upset stomachs). I hobble-walked and hobble-jogged the last ten miles, counting every mile going by, and looking forward so much to the end. The second half felt five times longer than the first. But one stride at a time.

Eventually and wonderfully, The Mall appeared around the last corner and the crowds lining the route were cheering and shouting and encouraging us on, empathising with the pain and strain on our faces. The atmosphere was fabulous, especially at this late hour when the strugglers and stragglers were limping in, so there was extra loud and emotional cheering and clapping for us exhausted backmarkers.

At a fairly unimpressive five hours, 12 minutes, I ran triumphantly over the finish line, under the winning gantry and felt absolutely fine. I'd done it. I hugged a woman who was crying and felt relieved; glad it was over and only slightly knackered. My ankles and knees hurt a bit, but all in all, considering I was not especially fit and not a particularly natural runner and not really built for streamlined efficiency, I did alright. I had my silver foil blanket, my medal and a huge grin on my face. Another one ticked off the list. But never again! Although... never say never.

The point is, though, that from that first day of training on the 4th of January, unable to jog for half a mile, I completed a Marathon on the 26th of April. Training one day at a time and running one mile at a time, I achieved my stretchy goal one step at a time.

*   *   *

On our boat in the round-the-world yacht race, one of our mantras was **Keep Scratching Away**, meaning every inch counted, every nautical mile, every action, every day, and every watch; never giving up until we reached our goal. Immense achievements can be realised just one step at a time... climbing Everest, sailing 60,000 kilometres around the world, skiing 1000 kilometres to the South Pole, and rowing the Atlantic. Single steps are positive, actual acts of progress. Put them together and you can get to your destination, if necessary surviving one hour at a time, particularly when the chips are down.

As a sailing team we persevered with courage and resolve and we never gave up - not even around Cape Horn when we were four crew down, 3000 miles behind after our second medical evacuation and being encouraged by Sir Chay Blyth and the Race Office to quit. Our sponsor, David Chapman, sent us the following message during the race:

> *"When you think you are running on empty, there will generally be a little more fuel left in the tank for when you really need it... Don't look at the big picture: it's the small steps you grind out one by one that get you there."*

He was an astute and insightful man. And here is a message we received from one of the race fans: *"Anyone can give up; it's the easiest thing in the world to do. But to hold it together when everyone else would understand if you fell apart, that's true strength."* It is amazing what you can achieve when you try. How many times have you looked back and thought, "Wow, I did that?!" Never give up, keep scratching away, one step at a time.

Paula Reid

Chapter 4

Love Life

You don't have to spend £50,000 or trek to the South Pole to have an experience, adventure or live life to the full. Living a full and happy life is not about being super rich or being a super hero. Like my wild swim in the local creek, there are memories to be made and moments to appreciate on no money, with no time, no kit and no special powers! No excuses either. Easy, free and fun adventures are everywhere and they are allowed to be innocuous and just plain silly. Embracing the mess involves letting go, reigniting the child within you and loosening up a little to love life.

One of my favourites is sleeping outside occasionally, even at home. I bring down my pillows and duvet and set up a camp in my back garden. Grown-ups aren't meant to sleep in the garden. As children we used to make camps and for many of us, those halcyon days spent mucking about, making camps or hides, getting filthy and climbing trees, comprise our favourite memories, but then we stop doing these delightful things and get serious. We become self-conscious and, driven by adult peer pressure, turn into sensible and sombre citizens.

Sleeping outside is a mini-adventure. It's not every day, especially in the UK, when you sleep under the stars and then go into work the next day harbouring the secret. It's wonderful to sleep in the fresh air, without a tent even, occasionally rousing to turn over and steal a quick peek at the stars or moon, then wake with the sun-rise and dawn chorus in a very natural way. It's a simple one to make happen and yet we don't do it because we get stuck into our habits and norms.

If you always eat the same foods, shop at the same shop, catch the same bus, watch the same type of film, meet the same people, you will stop noticing and slide into habit and comfortable routines, where your imagination goes to sleep, your senses dull and your mind quietens. "Loving Life" is about sitting up to take notice and re-engage with your life, loving and living it to the full - including the small and silly, innocuous and pleasant stuff: how you sleep, what you cook, where you shop, which films you choose to watch, what you typically do on a Sunday morning, how you get to work, and which sport you play. With some creative thinking, or an innovative, fresh approach, you can do something completely different in your day to day activities. A mini-adventure re-engages you with living life to the full and being fully present. Loving Life embraces the fun that can be had.

I use my "Live Life to the Full" bucket list to encourage my child out now and again, the child within me, that is. My list contains a mixture of tough challenges and eccentric events, impressive expeditions and whimsical "want-tos," because to me they all contribute towards a full and happy life. I have sought out or been persuaded to participate in some crazy activities, the sorts of things you may see on any bucket list, and here are some of the more entertaining ones.

* * *

The World Bog Snorkelling Championships

Legend has it that the crazy idea of holding a World Bog Snorkelling Championship started in a pub (where else?!) called the Neuadd Arms near Llanwrtyd Wells in deep Wales where the locals and regulars brainstormed ideas for raising money and potentially bringing tourism into town. Their objective was to create one new event every year and in 1980 the first *"Man versus Horse Marathon"* took place. There are now 13 events staged in Llanwrtyd Wells including stone-skimming championships, world mountain bike chariot racing championships and the world bog snorkelling championship. I fancied a go at the Bog Snorkelling and twisted Alex's arm to do it with me.

The Bog Snorkelling takes place in the very thick, black, peaty Waen Rhydd bog where the locals cut a trench 55 metres long. The event is held in the summer - on the August Bank Holiday - which makes swimming in a trench of water sound positively refreshing, but the bog itself is black and cold. The rules - yes there are rules! - are that you have to complete two lengths of the trench, without using a conventional swimming stroke, and wearing a mask, snorkel and flippers. There isn't much room to use the arms anyway, so essentially it's a "doggie-paddle" style of swimming powered by flippered legs. This sounds quite easy, but in reality 55 metres is a decent distance when you have to keep your head down, you can't see, it's blooming cold and all your oxygen is coming through a narrow, plastic tube. Then there's the added pressure of hundreds of people watching and shouting.

Most people compete in a wet-suit, but there is a fancy dress category...

I had to compete in this category of course. I couldn't "just" do bog snorkelling - that was way too ordinary! And I convinced Alex likewise. The main issue here was deciding what to wear that was comfortable yet had bog pulling power. I knew that once we were in the bog, all that would show was our backs and heads, so I needed a costume idea that highlighted the back and that would look quite cool sailing down a peat bog. I had visions of prehistoric fish, dragons and Stegosauri so devised a fictional creature called "The Clapham Water Dragon." We created spines of angular plates with pieces of 7cm thick green foam, 2m x 2m square, using a bread knife to carve out the backbone of our costumes. These we decorated to look like an ancient water creature, with green scales and streams of red and green weed made out of lighting gel sheets. We also bought fish hats with fins and tails that stuck up once your head was flat down in the water. It was a good look.

Once in Wales we joined most of the other competitors to pitch our tent on the local cricket field. With finishing touches on our Clapham Water Dragons done on the veranda of the cricket pavilion, we donned our wellies, grabbed fins, mask and snorkel and swayed off with hundreds of others towards the bogs. Our fish hats and long foam spine backs stole the show as they dragged behind us looking prehistorically majestic. At the bog, we signed in among much chatting and laughter; most competitors were in wetsuits and were bemused when they caught sight of Alex and I in full-on costumes. It was a chilly day on the exposed peat bogs of Wales and I wasn't looking forward to plunging into the trench; apart from my foam spine and welly boots, I was only wearing a pair of green pants and a t-shirt.

When it came to our turn, we drew quite a crowd, and a forest of cameras were primed to record the inaugural event of the Clapham Water Dragons swimming the bog. I was in first and it was freezing. The water was so peaty that when I looked through my goggles underwater, I could only see orangey-brown haze. Visibility was zero. There was no way to navigate using vision. My heart was pumping. Everyone was watching and cheering. I felt the pressure to perform for the crowds build as my lungs grew tight. They counted me down... I launched off, smiling around my snorkel. It was one of the funniest things I had ever done.

As it turned out, Alex and I came second in the fancy dress category. Only second! I was disappointed – what could be greater than Clapham Water Dragons? Two girls had swum the bog as a pantomime horse! I don't even know how the one at the back managed to breathe...

That night was one of the best spontaneous drunken dancing nights ever. I think the craziness of the day had gone to our heads and we were feeling oxygenated, liberated and

*speedy*hen
quality, delivered.

AMY LOU
58 ROCKBOURNE ROAD
SHERFIELD ON LODDON
HOOK
HANTS

RG27 0SR
UNITED KINGDOM

36913084

SPEEDYHEN.COM RETURNS
PO BOX 48
WESTHAM
EAST SUSSEX
BN23 6WB

Thank you for placing your order with Speedyhen.com! Should you wish to make a return please state the reason for return below and send your item(s) back to us at the above address.

Reason for return...................

Order ID: [23056354]   Order date: [07/11/2021]

UPC	TITLE	QTY
4002725974532	HOPPER DELUXE DIARY 2022	1

Thank you from Speedy Hen for your order.

Need help? Get in touch with us via contactus@speedyhen.com

celebratory. The pub was heaving with successful, bonkers bog snorkelling converts. It was a wild night and we danced like no-one was watching, inhibitions having been cast off in the bog. It had been a surreal, loving-life day which turned into one of those crazy, loving-life nights...

* * *

The Haxey Hood

The world calendar is peppered with eccentric, cultural and iconic events and Britain is a top destination for hosting the madness that plays out once a year in various pockets of the country. Cheese Rolling is one of the better known events and one that I haven't actually taken part in myself because I just know that my legs will run faster than my body can handle and I will end up tumbling out of control down the steep hill, probably smashing bones, sheep and other people on the way down. Then there is the bog snorkelling and Man versus Horse Marathon already mentioned, plus plenty of other crazy events hosted in the UK - the birdman of Bognor, bathtub racing, barrel-rolling, worm-charming, egg-throwing, nettle-eating, wife-carrying, pudding races, mud races, Santa races, snail races, lawn-mower races, wheelbarrow races, tiddlywinks, marbles, gurning, shin-kicking, toe-wrestling, and so on. What a crazy, mad, brilliant world! Love it.

"The Haxey Hood" is one such eccentric event with a long, eccentric history. It's essentially a giant rugby game played out between four pubs and two Lincolnshire villages in the North of England. The back story is that 700 years ago Lady de Mowbray was out riding when a gust of wind blew off her hat (hood). Thirteen farm labourers ran about trying to catch it and she named the one who handed it to her Lord of the Hood. The labourer who had caught the hat but had been too afraid to present her with it was named The Fool. On the Twelfth Night of Christmas the story is replayed, starting with the Fool reciting a poem before being set on fire in front of Haxey Parish Church. The Fool finishes with the words:

> *"Hoose agen hoose, toon agen toon, if a man meets a*
> *man nok 'im doon, but doant 'ot 'im."*

Which basically translates as: Pub (public house) against pub, town against town, if a man meets a man, knock him down but don't hurt him. Just like rugby, then.

Before the main event, there is a light version played out for the children and then one for the women. In the middle of an old potato field, a hessian sack "hood" is thrown out and the children (or women) run and scrum with it to the touch line, which is a lane that runs the length of the field. I watched the children's game and cheered them on, killing time for the main event. I had already vowed to myself not to take part in the women's event; I was waiting for the real thing! However, when the game master started the women's game, it was like a red rag to a bull. Well, literally it was a red rag, but I became the bull. I charged for it, full of passion and power, determined and fierce, incredulous that I was taking part, let alone behaving like a fully-committed, testosterone-filled All Black! Where did that come from?! I won the women's event.

Back to the middle of the frozen potato field and now there were hundreds people waiting to take part in the full edition of the Haxey Hood. There were 13 marshals representing the 13 original labourers (known as Boggins) in hunting pinks controlling us, and whenever the giant scrum (called a sway) collapsed they would blow a whistle and make sure we all stood up again, before kicking off play once more. The sway was huge, comprising a few hundred people, mostly men, in a pack of bodies; sweating and surging against each other in a two-way push towards one of the villages.

Steam rose off the scrum as it pressed and heaved for hours. It was an uncontrollable force, like an overpowering crowd swelling at a football match or rock concert, and potentially quite dangerous. I was slightly fearful a couple of times as I lost control of my own body in the midst of the roaring beast. When I felt panicky, I could sometimes manoeuvre to the outer edge of the pack where the pressures were lighter and there was room to get the breath back, but then I would push into the fray again to get the full experience of being in the thick of the action. It was hard to really know or see what was going on, but we did surge through people's gardens and I remember being pushed over garden walls, and once over someone's car. Crazy.

After over three hours, we seemed to be gaining momentum towards a particular village and a particular pub. Then it was like a tug-of-war when one team suddenly gets the drive going their way and the other team loses its grip. There was a roar, a surge of determined energy, I saw the landlord of the pub reaching out across the scrum, stretching desperately to grab the hood, to end the game. He got it! There was a cheer. We were bloodied and muddied, steaming and sweaty, bonded and full of bravado. In jeans, boots, rugby shirts and mud, with aching muscles and steaming bodies, we all piled into that pub, shook hands, clapped each other on the back, hugged and drank beer. What a great way to spend the start of the year!

* * *

Being a Film Extra

How many people have "being an extra in a film" on their list of things to do before they die? And is it for the fame or the money or the fun? Because if it's for the fame, they are wasting their time! When I have "acted" in a film, I pause it for the scene I think I'm in and then really focus to try and spot myself... and hope it's not been cut. There is no fame and we are called "background artists" in that our job is to blend into the background so we don't draw attention to ourselves. The money isn't a huge incentive either. But I LOVE being an extra because I do it for the love of it. The random, "guess what I did today" fun.

I now freelance for a living and can often be available at the last minute for a day's shoot. Most extras agencies won't take you on unless you are genuinely free to go to castings at short notice and on any day. One day I'll be running a high-power corporate session with a team of directors of a blue-chip company wearing my business suit and professional smile; then at 0300 that night

I will be running and screaming through the City to escape from a giant flood because the Thames Barrier has collapsed. It's a whole other world.

First you get a phone call or text asking for your availability for a casting. If you are available you get pencilled in and have to phone the agency after 1700 the day before to find out exactly where to go and what to wear. In the meantime, you do start to feel a little frisson of excitement wondering what the film is (and let's face it – how BIG a film it is), who might be in it and what sort of part you will be asked to play.

For example, I was delighted to be booked for two days to do *The Bourne Ultimatum*, the latest in the Bourne trilogy – and to learn that the main actor, Matt Damon, would be there at the shoot. We were to meet at Waterloo Station at 1000 wearing "autumnal clothing." This was one of the best briefs because I often had to be up at four or five in the morning to start early when locations were more deserted or to get to a distant location or studio. Waterloo for me was a few stops on the tube and we were starting as late as ten o'clock because they wanted to get the commuters out of the way first.

I had often wondered whether crowd scenes used the general public who happened to be there or extras. It seemed a huge waste of money to pay for people in scenes such as the one at Waterloo station when there were hundreds there anyway. And can you actually stop the public from using somewhere like Waterloo station just for the sake of filming a scene? I found out that production companies DO pay for hundreds of extras because they can direct them, whereas the public they can't. So we had signs up in the station stating that we were shooting a film and apologising for the inconvenience. Most people stayed out of the way or didn't even notice because they were in zombie train travel mode. For the more intrepid, such as three girls who had nothing better to do, they just joined in. There were so many of us being directed through megaphones that another three slipping into the mix didn't make any difference.

On site we had to check in with a production assistant, take our booking slip and then queue in front of wardrobe to get our outfit passed or amended. I often get into trouble at this point! On this filming, I interpreted "autumnal" as rich, dark reds and greens and russets, colourful but muted colours. No, no, that won't do at all. The wardrobe despot frowned at me. What were you told to wear? "Autumnal," I meekly said, giving her my best "I'm only a lowly extra and you are the goddess of wardrobe," She glared at me and sent me off to the racks of spare clothing to get toned down. I ended up in a brown shapeless coat so it served me right for my cheeky artistic interpretation of the brief.

Once the excitement of signing in and getting checked by wardrobe is over, the rest of the day is mainly spent sitting around, eating, reading, chatting and waiting to be called on set. It's money for old rope really. Even when you are on set, you are usually standing or sitting around and chatting in between takes, while they are re-setting the camera for instance. There's also great catering. For early calls we get a full fry-up breakfast with tables groaning under cereals, bread and tea urns. On night shoots we have to be fed every four hours, which sometimes means getting "lunch" at two in the morning.

On set the trick is choosing someone who looks agreeable or entertaining to be near while hanging around with nothing else to do but talk. The time flies if you find an interesting extra, and drags when you find a show-off or wannabe: "I was acting with Robert Carlisle the other day darling, and he said to me..." But there are a lot of normal people in this extra life - housewives, students, retired gentlemen - who do just do it for the fun.

So next time you watch *The Bourne Ultimatum*, freeze frame the bit in Waterloo station and see if you can spot a 5' 9" blonde in a shapeless overcoat amongst the hundreds of others... it may not look like it, but she is loving life among the crowds of zombie commuters!

* * *

La Tomatina

My friend Tiffany and I discussed what would be the most outrageous and incongruent outfits to wear to a tomato throwing festival. We thought something white and something posh. So we bought second-hand meringue wedding dresses to wear... as if throwing tonnes of tomatoes at strangers in Spain wasn't going to be mad enough.

La Tomatina, the tomato throwing festival, is an annual event held in Buñol, eastern Spain and has been going since 1945, allegedly following an angry altercation which ended up with the combatants grabbing vegetables off a nearby farmer's market stall to throw at each other. This early and genuine version of La Tomatina was stopped by the police, but re-lived a year later by some locals who enjoyed the food fight. The police broke it up for several years in a row, but it gained momentum and popularity. It is now an established eccentric event on the worldwide festival calendar.

Four of us flew out to Valencia and had a mini cherry tomato fight on the plane as practice. I'm sure the air hostesses loved that.

That night we went out dancing until two in the morning and after grabbing a few hours of sleep, breakfasted in the hotel wearing our outfits where people stared and congratulated me on my wedding day. In Buñol square, little old Spanish ladies smiled and squeezed my hand with happy approval. Little did they know that far from being a nervous bride, I was about to go to war!

The place was heaving with people - about 20,000 of them - and 90% were men full of beer and Spanish machismo. I must admit, it wasn't easy being a blonde in an off-the-shoulder white wedding dress in a crowd like that and I began to think that the dress was not such a good idea. My friend Jerry lifted me up on his shoulders at one point and as well as being mobbed, we got interviewed by a TV station so he asked me to marry him. Daft man.

When the tomatoes came, it was havoc: 125,000 kilos of overripe Spanish tomatoes arrived by truck after truck, moving slowly along the main street. Men and boys sitting on top of the red heaps scooped them out and threw them at us and we threw them back and at each other. The air became thick red with flying tomatoes and everyone and everything got covered in scarlet tomato skin, pulp and pips. Each second I would have several tomatoes thud into my face and head – the ripe ones were fun, the unripe ones actually hurt and sometimes I had to duck down to recover from the ringing in my ears. Our other friend actually couldn't take it very long and hid in a church doorway.

We fought for an hour, then a cannon went off to signal the end and everyone immediately stopped. Just like that. Contenders with missiles in their hands ready to launch obediently put them down. The ground was half a metre deep in red slush. Rivers of red gloop oozed down the drains as locals lifted up the drain covers, plastic sheeting was taken off the buildings and fire hoses blasted everything down.

I ended up totally covered in Tommies, being a main target in my dress. I had tomatoes in my ears, up my nose and reacted to the acid with a red rash all over my skin. What a great giant food fight though - utterly childish, pointless madness and an experience I totally recommend.

* * *

The London to Brighton Bike Ride

With 27,000 riders, 54 miles, three big hills and lots of fun, the London to Brighton bike ride raises £4 million each year for the British Heart Foundation. And a few British hearts are put under strain during the ride, toiling up the hills in the heat; especially the big one at the end, Ditchling Beacon just outside Brighton, standing at 248 metres with a gradient of 1:4.

The first year I chose to have a crack at the London to Brighton, I had cycled just once all year and that was for one mile to a mate's house so he could load the bike and me onto a van for the Clapham start line. My tyres had to be pumped up at the last minute because my pump had rusted and I didn't know how to change gears.

I also decided to do it in fancy dress. It was for charity and I pictured lots of people in costume - a bit like the London Marathon which I had done earlier that same year. In my local fancy dress shop I looked through the racks of Victorian, Edwardian, animal, and military costumes to find something that wouldn't get stuck in the oily, rusty spokes of my oily, rusty Peugeot racing bike. "Sexy Traffic Warden" seemed just the "ticket."

As it turned out, I only saw two others in fancy dress and 26,997 in normal cycling gear - where was their spirit of adventure? I had the time of my life as so many other riders and spectators called out, or flirted, or just smiled and waved as they saw me. I got lots of comic quips about parking tickets and how long they were going to leave their bike in various pubs on route. I also became a reference point among the 1000s as people judged how they were doing against the traffic warden and phoned each other to "meet by the traffic warden." The outfit was such a hit that the next eight years of bike rides I dressed up in as many different costumes as I could find that were short, not too hot and enabled me to cycle 54 miles. My self-imposed rule was not to do the race in the same costume twice. From 1998 to 2013 I cycled as a nun, nurse, fairy, angel, schoolgirl, gladiator, Superwoman and Wonder Woman. The nurse's outfit looked great but was made of PVC and the temperature that year was 86 degrees, so you can imagine how much I sweated. Salvation was given along the way with spectators squirting hoses and water pistols to cool us down and then I went straight into the sea at Brighton for a desperate cooling off. I also got an interesting sunburn pattern on my legs the year I wore fishnet tights!

(Talking of interesting suntans, my best one was when I went to the British Grand Prix at Silverstone on my birthday. My sister had painted a Union Jack flag on my face which got me on TV but when I went to wash it off I realised that no amount of scrubbing would remove the pattern. The sun had burned through the red and blue stripes but reflected off the white. I was left with just the white stripes against the background of a burnt red face. Not only that, I had a job interview the next day... to be a primary school teacher! I got the job.)

Maybe cycling 54 miles in a crowd of 27,000 amateur, wobbly cyclists in 86 degrees is not on your list of things to do before you die, but it was seriously good fun. The cycling turned out to be pretty easy with good humoured banter all the way. We also made sure we kept the calories flowing throughout the ride with bacon butties within an hour of the start, a pint and a burger at the half-way point, cream cakes and tea made by the Women's Institute in a field a bit later and an ice-cream at the top of Ditchling Beacon. There were fields of poppies along the top of the South Downs, beautiful scenery all the way and a hero's welcome along the Brighton seafront - all in the name of charity.

It's a winning formula: sunshine (usually), exercise, lots of food, a medal and money for a good cause. Hurrah! Loving life.

* * *

The World Body Painting Championships

I am always on the lookout for new adventures and experiences and I found one that intrigued me in an article in an in-flight magazine, the World Body Painting Championships in Austria. The photos looked very cool and on a whim I looked it up online. The website depicted beautiful lakeside scenery as a stunning backdrop to the most amazing and creative body art and I was pleased to find cheap package tickets for only 60 Euros per person including three nights in an Austrian lakeside hotel, tickets to the four-day festival and free entrance to the grand ball in a castle in the mountains overlooking the town. This was a "no brainer." A cheap break in a beautiful location, attending an event that promised to be original and entertaining. Once again, Alex agreed to be my chaperone on a crazy adventure while Mum was convinced we were going to a naked sex and drugs festival. In actual fact, it was a fabulous "trip" full of highs but no drugs and I am very glad I booked it on a whim (go for it!).

We flew out to Klagenfurt and after a breath-taking train journey, came to our Austrian chocolate-box hotel on the Worthersee Lake, with its balconies bursting over with geraniums and pink, white and mauve petunias. We could swim in the lake as the shallows were quite warm, and a boat which stopped nearby would take us to the festival each day. Perfect! On the first evening, we walked to the town hall where body-painting artists were offering their services free of charge for anyone who wanted painting for the ball. Alex and I were already in black tie – not bold enough to go to the ball in anything other than actual clothes – but others had their evening clothes painted on and the quality of the work was so incredible we found it hard to tell the difference between those who were dressed and those who were painted. To get into the spirit of the evening we had our faces painted with flames which danced up our cheeks and into our hair.

The ball was in a castle, perched in the mountains overlooking the town and the lake. There were acrobats, fire-eaters and trapeze artists, and everyone was either dressed or painted in the most fantastic manner. As uninitiated newbies, and not knowing what to expect, we walked around with big grins on our faces or our mouths hanging open, impressed, inspired, amazed and shocked at the incredible body-work that was strutting and dancing all around us. We even had the privilege to meet the top British artist Carolyn Roper, who went on to win the championship that year. My mum would have been surprised - she was perfectly normal, pleasant and polite; just brilliant at body painting. We had an incredible night in that Austrian castle, a rather dreamlike and bizarre night, but one that sticks in my mind. It was like being on drugs but without being on drugs. Or being caught in Alice in Wonderland meets the Sound of Music with some Cirque de Soleil from Vegas thrown in. My dreams that night were for once less eccentric than my waking moments.

For the next three days we visited the festival down by the lake. Each artist was allocated a gazebo and a theme or title to work towards within a set number of hours. We wandered for hours watching the artists' work unfold in each tent and experienced the build-up of tension as the clock ticked on. At the end of each contest, there was a show on the main stage with all the models parading their artists' work, followed by live bands playing in the evenings. There were different genres from day to day. On the first day - brush and sponge - the artists were typical body-painters like our friend Carolyn. On the second day the category was air-brushing and many of the artists were bearded Harley Davidson biker types. On the third day - prosthetics, demonstrating talent for creating aliens, robots and animals - the artists were film and TV make-up artists and designers, a whole different type of artist altogether. It was a strange and provocative fusion of people and production.

We took part in the amateur face-painting competition and came third. I had painted a cherry tree over Alex's face and we won a set of beautiful body glitters, stencils, glues and brushes which I used for parties back in the UK. It had been a strange event to attend, for people not into body painting, but totally wonderful. It was a fantastical, curious world and a little like Alice, I felt privileged to have got lost in it.

* * *

Z is for Zorbing

Sometimes when I deliver a talk about the things I have done, I deliver it like an A-Z quiz of events and activities. I cheat on X and talk about spending Xmas in Lapland husky sledding, but Z is genuine because Z is for Zorbing.

Zorbing is essentially rolling down a hill in a giant plastic ball. This was not one of the toughest challenges I have taken part in, but it was one where I laughed the hardest in the shortest amount of time. Alex and I chose to do a joint, wet zorb, getting into one together with a load of warm water. We tried to stay on our feet at the start but it wasn't long before we lost control and rolled down the hill, slopping around like we were in a giant washing machine. We laughed and screamed all the way.

Life is not about looking cool. Life is a ride, a giant roller coaster, and it is far better to embrace it and go with the flow, laughing and screaming all the way, than fight against it, trying to remain unaffected and unruffled. After screaming my way through a ride with my step-daughter at Thorpe Park, we girls jump off, rosy cheeked and bright eyed, shrieking with laughter and skipping to see our crazy photos in the booth - unlike the boys nonchalantly smoothing their hair back to its former precision. I wonder which of us had the most enjoyment out of the ride and who benefitted the most from the smiling, laughing, adrenaline and pheromone release? It is healthy to laugh. It's good for the soul, heart, hormones, physical energy, relationships, and life span. It's about loving life and sometimes just being childlike again.

I seek out mad activities as much as arduous ones. I find myself getting very serious when I am preparing for a big challenge. There is so much to do; and so much that is critical, that I have to focus, but in between these weighty experiences, I choose to rebalance with thrills that release the exuberant child. I love laughter. In seeking to live life to the full, I am also seeking joy. I love the feelings I get when I am fully living. I love life.

Chapter 5
To Seize and To Savour

"I no longer climb mountains, I walk through them," said a mature mountaineer recently at an adventure travel show. She went on to clarify that the quest to reach the summit faster, better or harder was no longer appealing; walking *through* the mountains was where the pleasure and satisfaction were at now. I love this distinction. I think we can choose to seize or to savour (or both) depending on our age, our mood, our energy, our goals and essentially what "living life to the full" means to us.

For me, living life to the full is about grabbing life by the horns and stopping to appreciate it. Both seizing the day, and savouring the moment.

In *Dead Poets Society* the English teacher played by Robin Williams passionately encourages his students to seize the day and live extraordinary lives. No wonder I cried when I watched that film years ago. I believe we should all make our lives extraordinary by living them fully, heartily and happily. We should live both boldly and keenly, go for it and delight in it, live in the present and be present, do more and be more... I choose to climb mountains *and* walk through them. They give me different pleasures. When I climb a mountain, I feel stretched and challenged, edgy and hedonistic. When I walk through them, I feel peaceful and awestruck, nurtured and eudaemonic (literally translates as "good spirited"). This is why I take on huge challenges such as skiing to the South Pole - seizing the day, as well as taking the time to stare up at a tree - savouring the moment.

Having enjoyed the beauty of living in the country and the buzz of living in London, I now live on the South Coast of England and when I return home from a day in town or days spent inland, that first view of the sea still feeds my soul every time. I feel a surging of joy and delight and then a calming peace washes over me. I enjoy the sea in all its states and seasons: when it's calm and glittering, when it's blowy and lumpy, challenging the heeled over yachts, and when it's crazy and tempestuous, crashing over the sea walls of our local bay, reaching heights equal to the top of the street lights. The seascape where we live provides us with year-round drama and we live alongside one of the busiest stretches of water in the UK – right on the Solent, with the Isle of Wight on our doorstep. There are yachts, cruise ships, cargo ships, tankers, tug boats, aircraft carriers, ferries, hovercraft, windsurfers, kite surfers, hydrofoiling moths and three circular Napoleonic Forts. There is always something happening; something to stop and stare at, even if it is just the weather, playing its part in the grand drama across the horizon.

I have been lucky enough to appreciate the sea from my own back yard; ride the seas on a round-the-world yacht race and explore the sea under its surface, diving and snorkelling. When I was younger, I spent hours and hours in the sea, swimming underwater as much as possible, with a cheap snorkel and mask set. I loved, and still love, the world under the surface. I take pleasure in blocking out the world above, deadening the noises of the seaside towns and swarming beaches, to dip down into my cloistered, watery biosphere. I revel in the feeling of buoyancy or fighting against it to delve further down, the pressing nature of the water all around me, the quiet thrumming and bubbling in my ears, the intimacy of poor water clarity yet the expansiveness of being in the sea. I am happy out of my depth and with cold darkness beneath me.

Happy in murky English waters; anything else is a bonus. I have dived on the Barrier Reef, in the Red Sea and off Belize in the Blue Hole, three of the best dive sites in the whole world, and I have savoured every minute of it. I have swum with manta rays and turtles, cage-dived with great white sharks, "bumped into" sharks on reefs and gotten a nose-bleed among bull sharks in Belize, but surprisingly one of my favourite experiences was swimming with seals off Kaikoura on the South Island of New Zealand.

Three of us had just been whale watching off the coast and swimming with wild dolphins in the open sea and I thought my day couldn't get any better. As we sauntered along the Kaikoura seafront, thinking of buying some langoustines off a fishmonger in the layby, we were offered a cheap deal to swim with seals, and although this wasn't something we had intended to do, we seized the opportunity to give it a go. I had low expectations - seals are such lumbering, smelly creatures as they sit and snort on the rocks, yawning and stretching in brown fat laziness. However, once I slid underwater, they danced a ballet, pirouetting and cavorting all around us, curious and playful, interactive and inquisitive, charming and friendly. The clumsy shuffling was gone; they were graceful, beautiful and sleek in their natural element and I was caught, childlike in the moment, mesmerised and almost wishing I was one of them. I experienced a connection with them down there, especially when they swam right up to my mask, nose to nose, and gazed with their liquid saucer eyes - right into my soul, it seemed. Their faces were beautiful - sleek skin, striking whiskers, velvety nostrils, and huge, round, limpid-blue eyes. They were gorgeous creatures, so ungainly on land and yet sylph-like under the surface. I was delighted that we had seized the chance to experience such a haunting and remarkable encounter.

There are so many enthralling natural wonders just begging for us to savour, to stop and stare at: there is inspiration all around us, in the tiny and in the infinity; in the sea, the moon, the stars; thunderstorms, sunrises and sunsets; dolphins, mountains, dew, frost and snow, fields of lavender, volcanoes, low lying mist, fire, spider's webs, bluebell and beech woods; the Southern Lights viewed from a boat in the middle of an ocean. I remember sailing one night on such a calm and still evening that the sea was like an ebony mirror and the stars were reflected perfectly in the inky surface; we were ensconced in deep blackness and glowing constellations, above and below and all around us. It was like we were sailing in an airship, suspended within the night.

I have chosen to purposefully and consciously seize and savour the world, and sailing gives us entry into some of the most extreme and delightful experiences on this diverse planet, experiences both invigorating and meditational. I have sailed through the Bay of Biscay, the Bass Straits, the Atlantic, Pacific, Indian and Southern Oceans, across the Labrador Current, the Gulf Stream, the Agulhas Current, the equator, across the doldrums, past the icebergs and the Bermuda Triangle. The sea was always in full glory, bountiful in providing a rich variety of moments beautiful and dramatic, pleasing and downright dangerous! I have sat on the bow of the boat with my legs dangling over, mesmerised by schools of pilot whales, giant humpbacks and pods of dolphins leaping and twisting off our bow wave. Watched flights of flying fish skim and bounce in synchronised skeins as the boat roused them into flight. At night dolphins torpedo alongside the boat leaving trajectories of phosphorescence. I have stared up at the albatross wheeling above us with their long, slender wings effortlessly riding the air, and I have laid on my back, with my head upside down over the side, staring at the waves chasing and riding each other, racing the boat.

Without light pollution, sailing grants access to the purest night skies. More stars than I ever imagined are strung out there; the Milky Way - a dense band of brilliance; the Southern Lights - shimmering curtains and clouds of green, indigo, purple, yellow and red.

* * *

Equally pleasing and extraordinary to behold are less natural wonders such as the Taj Mahal, the Pyramids of Giza and Machu Picchu. These outstanding sights sit magnificently within exotic landscapes: the hot Indian intensity of Uttar Pradesh; the dusty desert and hustle of Cairo; and the steaming jungle-clad Andean mountains threaded with Inca footpaths. While visiting these renowned wonders of the world, I have been awed and overwhelmed by their grand designs and architecture, their artificial beauty and the extravagant visionary aspirations that they uphold so spectacularly. These magnificent temples celebrate human vision and endeavour. Each beautiful in form, though so very different from one another: the geometry of the Pyramids, the pastel elegance of the Taj Mahal and the almost primeval power of Machu Picchu rising out of the jungle in dominating force.

Completing the Inca Trail to Machu Picchu gave me a big challenge to seize - mountains to ascend at altitude - and plentiful moments on route to savour - temples and views to meditatively appreciate. This trip was about climbing the mountains *and* walking through them, involving physical effort and mental tranquillity, both life-enhancing and enriching. Before departing for my trek, posters in the Cuzco agencies advised: *"Take only photographs and leave only footprints"* and as we wander over our fragile planet, it's a necessary reminder. If we do take only photographs (and sometimes the locals don't even like that) and leave only footprints, we are still leaving too many footprints on the Inca Trail so trekking has been restricted. The gentle paths and stone steps are getting worn by modern pilgrimages and now "only" 500 people are permitted to start the trail each day, including all the guides and porters.

On booking my trip, I was told there would be 17 of us in the group. Eleven "gringos" (including a couple of Germans we nick-named the "Schumacher Twins" because they shot off at a pace no one else could match and always arrived first at every camp and lunch spot), four porters, "Big Chief" in charge of logistics and Kenny, our fabulous guide. Kenny was a star. He was short, dark and wiry and spoke with difficulty as he had been involved in a climbing accident six years before which killed his girlfriend and left him severely debilitated. It was only thanks to luck that he survived, with several broken bones and traumatic head injuries. He was a great orator though; entertaining, informative and with a good sense of humour.

From Cuzco we caught a bus for two hours to the start of the trail, stopping off at a dusty little town called Ollantaytambo where we bought two crucial aids for our challenge - walking sticks and coca leaves. Cocaine comes from coca leaves and chewing them allegedly dispels altitude sickness. With a small pack on our backs, a walking stick in one hand, a few coca leaves in our mouths, trepidation in our stomachs and slightly disquieting thoughts of the challenge in our heads, we set off on our first steps of the 43 kilometre, four-day trek. Forty-three kilometres in four days doesn't sound much, but it was the Andean undulations at altitude that were giving us cause for concern.

Day One was actually very easy, except it got incredibly hot and as we burnt, we began to look like sun-dried tomatoes. After a couple of hours of walking, we stopped at a stunning spot for lunch - a grassy plateau overlooking the Urubamba River, down in a valley with steep slopes all around. Cook served us with soup, cheese salad, cold pasta and fruit salad, all washed down with a cup of mate de coca, a brew made from coca leaves. Life couldn't get much better than this.

We walked on in the afternoon for another four hours, covering about ten kilometres at quite a leisurely pace. There were a few steep bits but the main problem was the burning sun until it dropped behind the mountains at about four and relieved us all. En route we bought bottles of water from local ladies and chewed on our coca leaves. We mostly walked through eucalyptus and cedar trees along a flat, gritty path. It was a tranquil and pleasing day and didn't tax us greatly.

That night we stopped at a cluster of about ten huts. The porters had already put up our tents - this was positively glamping in my book - so we grabbed a mattress, dumped our stuff, had a very quick wash at the village stream and then settled around a table with the dogs, chickens and chicks, drinking beer and eating a huge basin of popcorn. Again we had a very good meal of soup, rice and chicken, local sweet-corn and mashed potato (one of my favourites!). Over dinner we chatted and got to know each other, but at eight-thirty thunder and lightning broke out all around us and we were soon in our tents in the middle of a raging storm. It was quite cold at that altitude even with thermals and other clothes on, and the tent shook as gusts of wind carrying lashes of rain thrashed the fabric.

Day Two on the four day Inca Trail is notoriously hard. Uphill all day, climbing from 3000 to 4215 metres; 1200 metres in one day at high altitude where even the fittest get short of breath. We knew it was going to be hard and we were dreading it. The rainstorm had cleared and we were woken up at 0500 by the porters with a cup of tea in bed which was very much appreciated and a perfect way to start the day. At breakfast we listened to tips from Kenny about tackling the big up: slowly and steadily; don't stop too much; climb in zig-zags when it gets too steep; and inevitably you will get there. One step at a time. Tips I have been using ever since.

We set off at 0620 when it was still nice and cool, with our little backpacks, and climbed and climbed and climbed for four hours. It was hard. It was mind over matter. Breathing was short and our legs were like jelly. We had our sticks to help us, but boy it was challenging - a bit like running the marathon. And you know how sometimes a song gets stuck in your head? Well on this one it was "She'll Be Coming 'Round the Mountain," in training for the marathon it was "Running Up That Hill" by Kate Bush, and in the book *Touching the Void* by Joe Simpson it was "Brown Girl in the Ring" by Boney M. Why always such awful songs?!

We paused frequently and briefly to take photographs and had a gorgeous pastoral stop just after some really steep, stone steps. There was a stream, a flat area of grass, sheep... and a flushing toilet! We collapsed in the sunshine and ate some M&Ms, knowing we just had one hour to go. There was a bit of snow on the ground but it was hot in the sun, and fresh at the high altitude. We felt invigorated and refreshed, loving life at that moment.

More climbing. More steps. Quad muscles screaming. No energy. No breath.

We forced ourselves on and up to the "saddle" – a dip between two peaks and the highest point of the Inca Trail, also known as "Dead Woman's Pass" (very encouraging). At the top the uphill effort felt piquant and worthwhile. There was a 360-degree panorama down the mountainsides in front and behind us, a snow-topped mountain arena piercing the blue cloudless sky all around, and hazy, verdant valleys in the far distance. As we sat and savoured, it was like an homage in devotion to life; a modern version of the ancient Inca pilgrimages of moral and spiritual significance.

After big hugs all round and photos, I slipped and fell on some black mud which made everyone laugh - porters and all! "Post-traumatic hysteric disorder" then kicked in which I find often comes after a hard time or serious concentration, and we had tears running down our faces; the feeling of release after such an effort making us light-hearted and light-headed. We practically skipped the next bit, down, down, down very steep steps for about an hour to our lunch site at 1200. By now we were very chuffed with ourselves; happy, hot and starving. Another great lunch was rustled up out of backpacks. I stuck my head in a stream because it really was very hot and I was really quite burnt.

As a group we decided to continue up the next peak to a further and better campsite away from most of the other trekking parties. So after lunch, we once more exerted ourselves and climbed up another shorter pass, stopping at a small ruin for a quick lecture from Kenny before pushing further up. Eventually we came to our second campsite – beautifully situated on the edge of a mountain with grass, a stream, a couple of huts and a sweeping mountain vista across our breadth of vision. It was pretty cold at 3600 metres, so we put all our clothes on, had popcorn and tea, chatted, ate and went to bed.

Day Three

Had quite a restless night; it had rained in the night and it was cold and damp, so my tent mate and I had swollen eyes in the morning! We had bad hair and face day look after a night's camping or sleeping outside, not very attractive. We had slept with our hats on too so it was a grim sight inside the tent that morning, but a magnificently beautiful one outside. We were delivered cups of tea again (such a good tradition!), and sat in our tent opening looking at the sun rise (0500) over the mountain tops. Probably one of the best early morning views in the world. The Andes, frosted with snow, touched pink by a rising sun.

My legs felt absolutely fine after all the exertion the day before, but my neck was pretty burnt. At 0600 Kenny took us up a large ruin which was very close to our campsite where he told us about the Incas and the history of the Inca Trail; we then walked along a flattish mountainside trail to another ruin and another lecture. I hadn't realised how many beautiful ruins there were en route to Machu Picchu, nestling quietly in the mountain creases, each stunning and interesting in their own right but overlooked in passing through to the great Machu Picchu just round the corner.

That afternoon we had a four-hour downhill trek which was almost as hard on the legs as the up; crashing down on the knees and pressurising the calves and thighs. The route was fun though - through jungle, fairy-moss and bromeliad-clad trees, all the time with the most breath-taking views. We stopped at one point very high up and had a sighting of Machu Picchu, still far away, and mountain upon mountain ranging around us. More down, down, down through cool jungle until we reached our third camp. After our last Inca Trail dinner, we groped our way back to our tents in semi-darkness with the birds singing their evensong and huge stag beetles thrumming around our heads.

Up at 0400 trying to get a head-start on all the other trekkers so that we might get Machu Picchu to ourselves. We knew the coachloads wouldn't arrive until later disgorging thousands of non-Inca Trail tourists into the ruins, but it was the other trekkers we wanted to steal a march on if possible. We tipped the five lovely porters, who were very bashful about being given money and thanked them warmly.

The plan was to get to the "Sun Gate" as early as possible to see the sun's rays spill out over the ancient site, bathing the ruins in golden, morning sunlight. So we dashed off at pace with the Schumachers at top gear for a 75-minute sprint. Unfortunately when we got to the sun gate, it was cloudy so we couldn't see a thing! Continuing to the ruins, walking faster and faster to get there first... Machu Picchu came into sight just as the white clouds were lifting and parting, wisps floating and weaving in and out of the old stone buildings. Beautiful. Magical. Mystical. It was a vast ruin, grey stone temples and terraces straddling the grass-covered mountains.

As Kenny told us, the Incas believed in the sun (Inca means son of the sun) and the moon as the two main influences in their lives. They also believed in three levels of the world: the sky and heavens where the spirits go, represented by the Condor, the earth for production, represented by the Puma, and the underground represented by the Snake. All were equally strong and important in their own way. At death the commoners were buried in the ground, and the nobles were mummified and entombed with possessions and servants needed for the afterlife. One high priestess was buried in the sun temple underneath a giant slab of stone.

They also believed in water purifying the soul - hence the 16 water fountains on site - and those who did not live at Machu Picchu made pilgrimages by walking the Inca Trail. The site wasn't rediscovered until 1911, when an American, thinking there might be a ruin somewhere in the mountains, asked some farmers to show him the way. A ten-year-old boy led him to an overgrown Machu Picchu. Two years later the American returned with an expedition and they uncovered this most amazing site. Lucky them.

After Kenny had edified and entertained us, we were free to wonder and wander, leave footprints and take photos. We hiked up Huayna Picchu which was *very* steep, but once on top we had a superb unbroken view in full sun across Machu Picchu and the surrounding mountains and valleys, where we stopped. And stared. We had seized the challenge by the horns, climbing *up* mountains for four days and now it was time to wander *through* them to savour the moment and just be. It's a beautiful world which inspires us to live life to the full. And as Robin Williams said: *Carpe Diem.* Seize the day. Savour the moment. *Make your lives extraordinary.*

Paula Reid

Chapter 6
Life is an Adventure

Life is an Adventure: a journey of discovery, an unusual or daring experience, a bold undertaking, an exploration to seek and therefore to find. These define both life and adventure, involving journeys of discovery and exploration; exploring the world and exploring the self. Our future life is *terra incognita*, unknown and unexplored; our unique and exclusive life paths are only ever trodden by us, and will always remain inimitable. We navigate through life with a rough map and an intuitive compass, but without really knowing where we will travel and where we will end up. We learn and discover along the way. We choose which paths to take.

We sometimes choose well-travelled paths, rutted with wear, and sometimes less travelled ones. The roads less travelled may "make all the difference" as Robert Frost's "Two Roads Diverged" poem suggests at the end. The untrodden path is about stepping away from the brochure, off the track, away from the tourists and embracing and discovering the "mess" of life. This necessitates a **just do it** and **one step at a time** approach, enabling us to **love life** and **to seize and savour** it.

I love exploring, adventure and discovery, both in the broader sense of life in general, and in the case of travelling - being in the true beating heart of a country, away from big brand hotels, tour guides and tired tourist sites, mixing with new, interesting people. Some of my favourite travelling moments are when I have been privileged to stay with tribes for a few days or weeks in Borneo, West Papua, the Amazon or with the Mongolian nomads. I "go local" when I am doing this and attempt to follow their path, without treading on their etiquette, rules or customs. I believe that I live life more fully like this; I have a more enriching and enlightening time living with them their way rather than rigidly sticking to my Western attitudes and behaviours, resisting the experiences flowing towards me. I try to shake off or leave behind my sheaths of inhibition, routine and habit, and immerse myself authentically in the real, local experience; allowing myself to be myself and go unplugged and uninhibited for a while.

But with travelling - as with life - you have to take the rough with the smooth. You can't filter the memories and keep all the good bits when you weave your rich tapestry; you have to take it all, and that's what living life to the full is about. The FULL bit means everything, the breadth and depth, the good, bad and the ugly, and when I choose to expose myself to different cultural experiences and be vulnerable and naïve, I accept the responsibility and the risk that I will see, hear or feel things that I won't especially like. The problem with stepping off the beaten path is that there is not so much of a safety net. The road less travelled is in the stretch zone.

I guess the alternative risk is that if I stick to the beaten path, I will have a more homogenous experience that has been sanitised and westernised, commercialised and approved, touched or shaped to appeal to, and be safe for, the masses. The beaten path is easier and one that I do travel often, but I have a longing to explore and discover the unknowns; unknowns which bring their own exciting, positive enjoyments and less pleasant challenges; unknowns in the geography, climate, culture, activities or in my own capacity to cope. The appeal is in not getting stuck in a rut but stepping out of the groove to explore the *terra incognita*.

I have worked in remote Indian villages, stayed with Dayaks in their long-houses in east Borneo, shared a bed with locals in the hill tribes of Sapa, North Vietnam and slept with the West Papuans around a fire in their cold straw huts. When travelling, I prefer to go off the beaten track to hill tribes and villages where they have rarely seen white people before; the conundrum in doing this is of course that you are inflicting your tourism upon these far-flung places, even though it is the very inaccessibility and lack of tourist infrastructure that appeals. At my most adventurous, I have no brochure, no tour guide, no map, no compass and no plan other than a dream. Paddling the Mekong, living with Mongolians in the Gobi Desert and trekking in West Papua were such adventures, native, intuitive, rich in exploration and discovery, and off the beaten track.

West Papua is the Western half of New Guinea, north of Australia, the other half being Papua New Guinea. It is bristling with jungles, tribes, mountains and rivers and took two of us four days of flying to arrive in the middle of West Papua at a village called Wamena in the Baliem Valley. Wamena is about as touristy as it gets in West Papua - even there I only saw two other non-locals, including a Swiss guy called Edine who we teamed up with to explore.

From this Baliem Valley "hub" - a marketplace with a few proper shops but mainly local tribespeople selling their home-grown produce – we trekked out into the mountainous terrain with a local man, his niece and nephew. This charismatic and charming family team were not tour guides, simply enterprising and opportunistic locals trying to earn some money. I don't think they had even been to where we trekked, but they had enough local knowledge and adaptability to look after us and guide us from village to village - there was essentially only one footpath connecting them all anyway - and it generally took a day of strong, pacey walking to get from one village to another. We trekked for over three weeks, rising up from the river valley over thousands of metres into the isolated jungle-clad mountains where there are no roads, tracks or vehicles, just the occasional

Mission Aviation Fellowship airstrip run by Christians and serving the local communities.

In this deep, green and remote place, villages with thatched huts accommodate several families. Many of the villages belong to different tribes and speak a variation of the Bahasa Indonesia language. The huts sit in pockets of cleared land, surrounded by primary jungle and sometimes enveloped by low clouds rolling in from the mountains in the afternoons. The villagers grow crops such as sweet potatoes on the mountain slopes, hunt birds with bows and arrows and collect firewood. There is no electricity, no generators or running water and they sleep around a fire when the nights are cold, huddling for warmth among the fleas and foodstuffs, rarely with blankets or clothes.

I am sure that most of them, especially in the more distant villages, had not seen a foreigner before. I am 5' 9" and Edine, my Swiss travelling friend, must be about 6'. We wore high tech, wicking T-shirts and trousers, walking boots and small rucksacks. The locals ranged from 4' to 5' in height, wore penis gourds or grass skirts, and instead of a camera and water bottle, might be carrying a pig under an arm, or an axe or bow-and-arrows slung over a shoulder. Sometimes we would meet on a path between villages, sometimes we would arrive at a village and ask permission to stay the night. Each time we met, there was a delightful moment as we made eye contact. There was no hostility, resentment or fear as far as I could make out, just a "sizing up," an assessment, and then a deep and personal connecting. They would look at us and we would look at them for quite some time, politely and interestedly, with patience and respect. Then perhaps the eldest male of the group would approach me or Edine, look us keenly in the eyes, clasp our hands in both of his and softly say "whah, whah" many times. It's a beautiful experience and these moments are the ones I feel most grateful for when I travel. I very much admired and delighted in their culture and the West Papuans we met were generally extremely kind, gentle and hospitable. My whole trip to West Papua was off the beaten track, off the map, off the grid and unplugged from technology, and I trusted in the locals to keep me safe and fed, and trusted in the experience to provide me with a brilliant journey of exploration and discovery, with some excitement and risk. A true adventure by any definition.

Backpacking and not staying in 5* hotels is one way to draw closer to a country for a more authentic local experience. While backpacking around Vietnam with a friend, Michael, we enjoyed the tranquillity of the rice fields in the Mekong Delta, the crazy worlds of the Chu Chi war tunnels and Cao Dai "Holy See" Temple, busy and fast Hanoi and Ho Chi Minh cities, clothing workshops in Hoi An, the fortress at Hue, and the limestone karsts penetrating out of Halong Bay. We had travelled light, staying in youth hostels and eating at local food stalls. The whole experience had felt rich with cultural immersion, steeped in traditional and modern Vietnamese ways, revealing worlds to us from the past to the modern day.

When travelling on local buses rather than tourist buses, walking freely without a tour guide, or sharing a local train carriage in third class rather than with the tourists in first class, we had our best times. Not necessarily our most comfortable or convenient experiences, but our most genuine and memorable ones. So taking that thought one step further, we discussed what we wanted our next trip to be. We had loved Vietnam. How then could we enjoy a country more by travelling, eating and sleeping with the locals; going off the beaten track, being among them and with them rather than observing them and paying them? Cycling, perhaps. Or walking. With a rickshaw or on a boat... We eventually settled on the fairly unique idea of finding a decent sized, interesting river and travelling like a local. One of my favourite Live Life to the Full adventures was born - paddling the Mekong in a dugout canoe.

A year later, Michael and I flew out to Bangkok and caught a bus across the Thai border to Phnom Penh, the capital of Cambodia. We had a rough plan. A very rough plan. And a large scale map.

The Mekong flows from the Tibetan Plateau through China, Burma, Laos and Thailand before running from the north of

Cambodia, through Phnom Penh in the south and out to Vietnam's Mekong Delta, with various tributaries joining from the mountains. I bought a map of Cambodia to look at where we could start and finish, wanting to go to the Angkor Wat temple in Siem Reap, but apart from that, happy to go anywhere. As I was poring over the map, a friend pointed out a small tributary river called the Srepok, with a handy local airport at Banlung in the north east of the country and a village called Lumphat not too far from that. *"Why don't you start there? You could fly in and paddle down that river and see how far you get?"* he suggested. And that's what we did.

I packed a tent, a rucksack of backpacking clothes and a few bits, which weighed my usual trekking weight of just less than five kilos. Michael's weighed significantly more and one day I found that he was carrying a bag of nails and screws! Michael knew my reputation and talent for being Little Miss Travel Light and Fast and was immediately defensive and embarrassed. Apparently he had packed them "just in case." He is a builder after all. I haven't stopped teasing him about it yet, twenty years later. Every time on that trip we had to do something practical, like cook or put up the tent, I asked him if he needed his nails and screws...

In Cambodia we stayed in Siem Reap and visited the Angkor Wat temple complex for a few days, where I felt akin to one of my fictional heroines, Lara Croft (it is where they shot some of the first Tomb Raider film) while wandering around the crumbling edifices being devoured by the jungle, entwined with creepers and tree roots. From Phnom Penh we caught an internal flight on a Twin Otter to Banlung airport in the north east. Banlung is a small town and here we managed to negotiate motorbike rides to the river, which was about two hours away on dusty, rutted tracks. With my backpack I rode pillion on a trail bike, bumping up and down behind a Cambodian youth, not 100% sure whether he understood where to take us and now and again grinning across to Michael who was having an equally dusty and fun time. Quite often I thought I would bounce right off the bike, and a few times we had to get off while they revved and pushed their way through the mud. This was already my sort of adventure. Wind and dust in my hair, not sure where I was going, trusting in the locals, loving it, laughing and carefree.

Towards the river, our two escorts kept looking at us to check what to do. I don't think they quite understood what we wanted, which was fair enough considering our daft plot. They started to look worried but we kept waving for them to ride on. We were looking for a village on the river; our map wasn't detailed enough to show any but we were pretty confident we would come across something, and sure enough we arrived at a very small, tribal village on the bank of the River Srepok. There were no roads or vehicles here, just pigs and chickens scrabbling about, so when four dusty strangers appeared on motorbikes, two with backpacks, we caused quite a stir. The whole village crept out of their huts to come and stare; the biggest and tallest of whom approached us and seemed to be the chief. We smiled. He talked. We didn't understand. He asked our escorts why we were there, but they didn't know either. There was a lot of talk between the chief, the bikers, the other elders, the chief's wife, and the rest of the village. They were looking at us and wondering what on earth we were doing there. We stood and smiled and waited for a chance to explain our quest. We had come to buy one of their dugout canoes. If they had any.

One of my favourite impressions of South East Asia is the engaging and delicate hospitality, peace and patience of the hosts. In a quietly dignified manner, the chief sat down with us on the dusty ground and together we drew pictures with sticks to create a dialogue. I am usually quite relaxed in situations like this and enjoy the challenge of communicating. There is a mutually binding goal of understanding one another, with respect and humility on both sides.

After about an hour, with many drawings, smiles and much laughter between us all, as the children pushed and shoved to see what we were up to, there was a dawning of comprehension; the chief suddenly seemed to understand. He exclaimed loudly and the village all shouted and nodded. He looked wise; we probably looked bemused and hopeful.

Beckoning for us to follow him, he led us through the village, along a path between some reeds and to the river bank. He pointed down, and there, nestling innocently against the river bank, was a dugout canoe. She was clearly a hand-made piece of craftsmanship, carved out of a single piece of wood. She looked sleek and balanced. The Chief looked at us hopefully. We grinned and nodded and gave him the international sign of the "thumbs up."

So far, so good. We had managed to get to the river, find a village and find a boat...The main adventure was looking likely!

It took us another hour, squatting in the dirt on the river bank, to explain that we actually wanted to buy the boat, we didn't want anyone coming with us and they wouldn't see the boat again.   This must have been the second big surprise in our negotiations. The chief probably thought that we just wanted a tour on the boat, or perhaps to go fishing with the locals, but to actually take the boat, without any escort and not come back, was quite a stretch of his imagination. Poor man. He remained so friendly and dignified throughout, but must have been completely baffled by our gesticulations as he desperately tried to understand us and give us what we wanted. But he stuck with us, as genial and polite as you could wish for, for the two hours it took for the deal to be sealed. Again, we suddenly got a beam of a smile and his face lit up as he realised where we were going with our request. He nodded and grinned. More thumbs up from both sides. We then had to negotiate a price.

Not knowing what the going rate was for buying a dugout canoe in rural Cambodia, never having previous experience in doing such a thing, we had brought with us an amount of local riel and US dollars. We figured that the boat must have taken a while to create - felling the tree, seasoning it in the river, carving it out, fine-tuning the balance of the thing and producing the two oars. It was their mode of transport and possibly their source of livelihood too. I'm guessing that next to their huts, it's the second most crucial possession in their lives. We scratched numbers in the dirt with our sticks. The chief was pretty clear on this point. He wanted $90, no more, no less, so that's what we paid for "The Srepok Drifter" and we shook hands on it. How exciting! Our made up adventure-challenge was now a reality. Whether we could actually paddle the river, achieve any distance and survive on our own without a decent map or satellite phone was still to be seen.

For the rest of the day there was much socialising, eating and drinking with the villagers. We were dragged on a tour of the village huts, as it turned out, to buy various items from them all! This worked out very well for us and made them grin and "thumbs up" a lot too; they must have been happy doing business with us. Making sure we spread the love and bought something from each hut we ended up with bags of glutinous or "sticky" rice (our staple diet for three meals a day for the next month), tins of sweetened condensed milk, tins of pilchards, coffee, a pot, two spoons and a dodgy bottle of bright yellow pineapple liquor. We were invited to stay with the chief and his family that night, and the exciting day finished with us sleeping on their floor, snuggled up with him and his wife, their children and the dogs.

Up with the sun the next morning, we packed our sleeping bags under the giggling gaze of dusty, sniffling children as they whispered and pointed at bits of our kit. We collected our shopping and rucksacks and headed down to our boat. Unbeknown to us they had been working on the boat overnight, filling the holes and making it more durable and watertight. Lovely people. We loaded her up, putting most of our kit in the middle and trying to look as confident and professional as possible in front of the whole village which had turned out to see us off. It was about 0700 and we were ready. It was time to commit to the river. The villagers were expectant, smiling and nodding at us in encouragement. I don't know whether our nerves showed. We gave them a last confident wave before stepping into the boat and sitting down. This resulted in a lot of laughter and shouting and waving at us. We had sat facing the wrong way!

Here we were, naively about to paddle down a river in Cambodia, and not even knowing how to sit in the damn canoe.

Just do it, though; one step at a time. I had already travelled with Michael around Vietnam, so we had some instincts for each other, but neither of us had ever paddled a dugout. We didn't know how far we would be able to go, or how fast we would travel. We didn't know what would happen if we had to stop in time to catch our flights home and get out of the jungle somehow. We didn't know if there were any rapids up ahead because our map was so basic, though there was a rather worrying picture of a waterfall towards the end of the Srepok, just before it joined the Mekong. We didn't know if what we were undertaking was going to be dangerous or impossible. My biggest worry was if we hit rocks or sank or came upon an obstacle such as a roaring waterfall, and ended up on the river bank with all our stuff, how would we cut through the impenetrable jungle and find our way to civilisation? Cambodia had a dark side in those days. They were still clearing land mines and there was talk of the Khmer Rouge operating in the mountains. We were truly off the beaten track, on the path less travelled. I was hugely excited at the prospect of our adventure, however, exploring and discovering and trying out new things; I was in my element. I was also going in with my eyes wide open. Life is an adventure, and while we weren't exactly stuck up **** creek without a paddle, we were sitting on a Cambodian river, with a leaky boat, two paddles and a bag of food, about to launch into the unknown.

On the sensible side of the equation, we continually evaluated the best way forward, both being practical and pragmatic. Michael was a solution finder and I was a creative thinker. He was easy going, I was driven. Michael was great at making and fixing physical things and I was great negotiating resources with the locals. I communicated not by speaking Khmer - though I did try - but through drawings and charades, happily acting out what we wanted or needed. I bonded especially well by playing with the kids, helping the women and smoking or drinking the local brew with the old men. As a local networking formula, it generally worked.

We were a symbiotic team, both capable travellers, able to pitch a tent, create and maintain a fire, cook, look after ourselves and look after each other. We had traveller's nous. We were fit and strong and willing to put in the hours and the grind on the oars. Michael steered from the back of the boat, I navigated and we both put in the muscle. We didn't scare easily and we'd generally packed the right kit (nails and all). We had two lifejackets with us and a basic GPS tracker. We'd bought local food, mostly rice, which should be easy to cook and filling and we were carrying some decent first aid equipment, purifying tablets, iodine and a water filter. We were savvy enough about navigating and river travel, albeit without much actual paddling experience, and we would be travelling with the flow, so we thought our speed would be decent. We were, on the one hand, very prepared and able; on the other hand, about to set off on a madcap adventure with no one really knowing where we were. Nuts or guts?!

The psychologist Mihaly Csikszentmihalyi is credited with researching and defining the psychological state of "flow." Previously it was generally known as being in the "zone" and most often used to describe creative or sports performance. Being in the zone, or experiencing flow, describes a state of optimum performance, where the mind and body are at one, fully engaged and present with the activity they are undertaking such as dancing, computer gaming, painting or running a marathon. The activity is typically challenging and requiring a decent level of skill, but still within the performer's ability. The performer will feel completely absorbed in what he/she is doing, not self-conscious or distracted, and is likely to lose track of time. Flow is generally considered to be a very positive, invigorating experience and takes you into the gentle stretch zone, beyond comfort but nowhere near panic.

The river was flowing in the right direction for us and after a couple of days we managed to catch the mental state of flow too. Gradually our troubles and cares from the life we had left behind in the UK dissipated and we were left with the singularly focused task of paddling. It was pleasant work. We paddled all day, often in our own worlds, sometimes listening to music but usually just letting our thoughts drift with the stream. The weather was perfect, very warm but not baking or burning and generally we had overcast skies and the humid heat typical of South East Asia. Michael wore a sarong and I wore a bikini top and shorts; he sat at the back, leaning against his rucksack, steering as necessary and I found it best to stand-up paddle at the bow. Maybe this was an early version of SUPing or stand-up paddling, but I found this position easiest as my oar was long and heavy and I found it hard to constantly lift it up over the side of the boat for each stroke. The boat was beautifully balanced for a hand-made dugout canoe (unlike the following year when we decided to try the same adventure in Nicaragua!) and I easily kept my balance, paddling down and along from the bow, changing sides as required.

The Srepok River was generally flowing smoothly and in the right direction, carrying us gently and inevitably towards the giant Mekong to our south west. It was about 30 metres wide, bordered each side by virgin jungle. We didn't see much civilisation at this stage of our journey, no locals or villages for days on end. This is from my diary on Day One:

Had dragon fly sit on our boat or oars now and again. Lots of bright blue kingfisher on the banks. Some fish eagles? Buzzards, sand pipits, and once, a couple of black monkeys. At night lots of ants, mosquitoes and some millipedes. Today rowed from 0700 until about 1400 when we pulled over in the shade and opened a tin of pilchards for lunch. Rowed for another hour after our stop and found a great sandy place to pull up for the night. Perfect. Mike 'caught a fish' which happened to jump into our boat! Set up tent, collected firewood, tried to cook 16 fish which we'd bought off a guy from his boat but they were foul, so gave up and chucked them away. Had rice and pilchards instead! Read our books by the fire, had pineapple wine and coffee, then went to bed about 2200. 'Fish Camp'.

Every day was pleasant and with a purpose, this was a seize and savour adventure. We would wake up with the sun rising and start a fire for coffee, while packing up the tent and washing in the river. The temperature was perfect, though at that time in the morning the river dip could be a little fresh and invigorating. After some housekeeping, we would sit together by the fire and slowly wake up and chat with a coffee and our daily breakfast - cooked rice with sweetened condensed milk - a bit like rice pudding, which we had cooked the night before and left to hydrate overnight. Whilst the day was still waking up and there was a peaceful air to the river, we packed our stuff into our loyal and patient dugout and pushed off from the bank, with Michael sitting at the back in his sarong, and me standing at the front, facing the new world and whatever the river would bring that day. We then got into the flow and allowed the river and time to pass us by. We were happy, confident and purposeful, making great progress and at ease with the world around us.

Typically we paddled for maybe four to five hours before pulling up on a bank, or more often just catching hold of some bamboo or a branch overhanging the river so that we could park up for lunch. We would then slide off again and paddle until about 1600, when we started to look for a camping spot for the night. Ideally this would be a sand bank on the river edge, clean and comfortable and clear from the jungle but ideally surrounded by bamboo - one, because I love the oriental elegance of bamboo, and two, because the big, dry stalks burned so well. Once we agreed on a campsite, we would row hard towards the bank and ram our dugout up as high as we could. By 2100 we would be just gazing into the fire and contemplating life, with trousers tucked into socks to protect us from the mosquito - the only pest in the whole, idyllic set-up.

It was a simple existence and we were at peace, yet accomplishing an adventurous challenge. We were definitely experiencing flow. Excitement was very occasional: buying fish or a machete or more rice, and on one night there was a most dramatic electric storm so we launched the *Srepok Drifter* into the middle of the river towards some rocks, holding onto them as we watched the lightning fork across the river horizon. For ten days we had idyllic paddling conditions and our plan made on the back of a fag packet had materialised into a perfect adventure. We were working hard but never exhausted or in pain. The only times that caused us some concern were when we came upon rocks, white water and rapids.

Firstly, the noise would worry us - the gentle roar in the background that got louder and louder as we drew nearer. Without any white water training, I was the navigator calling the route through and Michael steered according to my arm-waving. It would have been disastrous if we had fallen in and more so if we had lost our boat in the middle of the primary jungle. Not a great prospect. So each time I heard the distant roar of the rapids, knowing that I was responsible for navigation, I would get butterflies in my belly. Would we make it through or did this roaring herald a disaster? Each time we approached, we had to make a quick and unwavering decision to either go for it or bail out before we got pulled into the heaving and roiling white water. In every instance we determined to press on and navigate our way through. We twice hit rocks and nearly capsized, but managed to rebalance by shifting our body weight in quick response among the chaos, noise, rocking, spinning and water pouring in. Five seconds more, or one inch lower and I think we would have lost the lot.

Once we started to power through the rocks and white water, steering a course in our little dugout, adrenaline kicked in and I was thrilled that Michael and I were able to do this. We were a successful team. Sometimes you just have to have a go and do your best and then you may surprise yourself – we are all more capable than we realise.

However, on the map there was one picture of a waterfall on our river ahead. It had been worrying us since before we left the UK; we weren't sure whether it was a symbolic artist's impression to make the map look more interesting, or marking the spot of a real waterfall. It was drawn near the end of the Srepok, where our river met the Mekong, and initially we weren't even sure we would make it that far, but after ten days of paddling, we were heading quite rapidly towards the mighty Mekong. We even worked out that at our rate of rowing, if we put in the hours, we could possibly make it all the way to Phnom Penh in time for our flight... but first, we had the hurdle of the fictitious or ominously real waterfall.

As we drew nearer to the picture on the map, and nearer to the civilisation that the Mekong naturally attracted, we saw two huts on stilts on the left bank. Quickly deciding to pull in and ask about the waterfall, we rammed our boat up the bank and cautiously approached. The huts must have been ten metres high and looked a bit unwelcoming stuck up in the air compared with the random cluster of ground-based dwellings we had gotten used to along the river. We called up and a little girl poked her head around the doorway then disappeared crying. Not a good start. We waited, hoping that the usual Cambodian hospitality would emerge from the dark interior. After a while we were beckoned up by a shy lady and climbed up the vertical ladders with difficulty. We did the usual greetings, handshakes and bows, and squatted on their floor as the family looked quizzically at us. I don't think they understood where we had come from, never mind understanding our question about whether the waterfall existed or not because we were paddling the Mekong in a dugout canoe for the hell of it.

We showed them the map with the picture of the waterfall and mimicked rowing a boat and looking worried. We also drew pictures of rivers and boats and waterfalls and they nodded quite definitely and energetically at the mention of a waterfall. This was not encouraging. I got the impression that the husband had been fishing near there and knew it was dangerous. We thanked them and left, rather worried and uncertain as to what to do. However, there wasn't much option. There didn't seem to be any transport or roads nearby so we decided to proceed with caution. Paddling tensely with ears and eyes wide open, waiting for that distant roar, but it never came. After quite a few anxious hours we stopped for the night, fairly sure we had passed the place on the map. The graphic of the waterfall must have been for artistic purposes and the family we had asked about it were perhaps just generally worried about our journey. Phew! Waterfall-gate was over and we could concentrate on the next leg of our passage.

The following morning, we rowed towards quite a sight - the Mekong in full flow right across the end of our river. We were pleased and proud that we had made it thus far but the Srepok had been like a training ground for newbie paddlers; the Mekong was in flood; she was impressive, full-bodied and certainly not a river to be taken lightly. It was time to step up the challenge. The incredibly gratifying adventure had moved up a gear into a satisfyingly demanding expedition and with the confidence and skills we had garnered thus far, we joined the great Mekong. This was a much faster flowing river and having left at 1120 and stopping for a swim, we managed an amazing 37 miles that afternoon - twice the distance we achieved in a whole day on the Srepok.

Then, on just the second day of the Mekong, we hit trouble.

> *1045. Currently sitting in Police Custody! We rowed for two hours (15 miles) and then got picked up by the river police with guns. We're sitting in a dark hut with 40 people, one pig, a dog, some chickens, chicks, a cockerel and a lizard. The younger police officer took 40 minutes to understand Mike's passport – he's not the brightest.*

We were in custody for three and a half hours.

> *They gave us lunch and we tried to leave but they wouldn't let us. I had to go for a wee at one point and they followed me out, shouting, pointing their guns at me and refusing to look away as I squatted for the toilet. At 1300 a major and sergeant arrived with some border police from a town upriver called Stung Treng. The sergeant spoke quite good English, they introduced*

themselves and then said he wouldn't permit us to carry on because the river was too dangerous. He said the waters were very high and fast at the moment and even the locals didn't do what we were doing. Apparently a local Chief had seen us go past and phoned it in. The proposed solution was to go back upriver 50 miles to Stung Treng and catch the public Express Boat to Phnom Penh. We were gutted.

So we tied our little row boat to the police long-tailed boat and hitched all the way back with them which took until dark – about 1800. One policeman sat in our boat bailing her out now and again. The police were now very friendly and we stopped off to buy a bottle of local brew (rice wine?) which then got passed round all of us until we'd finished the bottle!

The sergeant offered to take us to Laos for the weekend (as he's in charge of the border, visas wouldn't be a problem) but we didn't have the time. We had a cunning plan.

The next day we hauled our dugout onto the roof of the Express Boat and sat waving goodbye to the whole of Stung Treng, police and all. Then we cheekily put our plan into action, getting off with our boat at the next stop - Kracheh - and carried on paddling towards Phnom Penh.

We paddled hard and for long hours towards the end, just so we could make it all the way. One day torrential rain persisted which was cold and unpleasant, but for the rest of the time we had warm, muggy air and occluded skies. We both got very brown, fit and slim on our diet of rice, and rice, and rice. Our only natural predator was the mosquito, which was doggedly attacking us. I always get bitten a lot despite the repellents and in a study one evening I decided to take a sample amount of skin versus mosquito bites to calculate how many I may have on my whole body. I took half a leg below the knee and counted 117 bites; I must have had a thousand or so in total. Michael also once had diarrhoea and I accidently gave him laxatives instead of Imodium, which I didn't confess to until a few days later when he finally got better!

On our last day - our final row into Phnom Penh - we felt rather sad to be finishing our home-brewed adventure. Moving at quite a pace, the end was coming sooner than we had expected. The current was strong, pushing us along, with little waves and the wind behind us. Blue sky, hot sun, perfect conditions to finish in. I stood up and rowed for the last time until it got too rough. We had just one bit of very choppy water to cross...

Launching into our last stretch of busy river, churned up with commercial boats, we were met with metre high waves. Here at the capital city, three rivers collude, and the water was both turbulent and hectic. We knew we had to row as hard as we could across to the other side at right angles to the traffic to avoid being in the shipping channels too long. The waves were coming in thick and fast, the wake from all the boats was creating more chop, and I was getting sloshed by a surge of water slapping the bow full on every 30 seconds. Mike was bailing for our lives.

In the middle of all this, we had a shouted debate about where exactly we were on the map, and where, therefore we were headed, so we decided to pull into the far bank to double-check before we continued or stopped. The waves were still pretty rough, even out of the main river channel, so once we pulled in, we were pounded and pounded against the side. We were both bailing by now and within seconds we were half full with water, realising the situation was nearly irretrievable. We couldn't stay there a moment longer, so we pushed off with difficulty. Unfortunately, the boat was soon pushed back against the shore, and with Mike bailing, I didn't have the strength on my own to get us away. Two more huge waves over the side and that was it - the boat went down!

There was nothing we could do. All our kit went down too. The boat sank but we could just make out the top edges of it under the waves as it rested on some reeds and bamboo. We got out, sank up to our chests in mud and rooted around underwater to grab our stuff, managing to find all our bags and cameras which we threw onto the bank where by now a group of concerned / bemused locals were gathered. A woman grabbed one end of an oar and pulled us up out the mud. Mike and I collapsed on the bank, covered in mud, with soaking cameras, money and passports and got hysterics. What an adventure!

Paddling the Mekong gave us a proper off-the-beaten track, unplugged experience, as we explored life Cambodia-style from our dugout canoe. Whether we call it an expedition or an escapade, it was definitely adventurous and in our quest to experience a country naturally, and to take the road less travelled, we had undertaken a journey of exploration and self-discovery, full of exciting uncertainty and bracing ambiguity. This was living life to the full; this crazy, unplanned, *terra incognita* adventure invigorated me; making me feel that I was fully living and by the same token making me feel fully alive.

* * *

Conversely, my trip on the Trans-Siberian was a less adventurous one, until I decided to step off the train and go solo and local in Mongolia. The Trans-Siberian - one of the classic railway journeys of the world - held a romantic lure and felt like a "must do" on a living life to the full list. I chose the Moscow – Beijing route which took me through Russia, Mongolia and China for 9000 kilometres on my own. It was a semi-packaged programme which rather went against my instinct, but what with the train tickets, the visas required and the formalities involved, I thought it best to book with a travel agent to ease the bureaucracy and free me from red tape to enjoy the trip.

It was good, quite interesting, easy to sit and watch the scenery go by, but a little dull. The initial excitement and romance of it was pretty much suppressed by the actuality of travelling for days on a train confined to a four-berth cabin, within a train carriage, within a train, ruled by very dictatorial and unfriendly provodnista (Russian train hostesses). We all enjoy different holidays for different reasons, and for me, the reality of this one was rather stultifying; an adventure for sure, but one that was constricting after a while. From Moscow to Beijing, we spent seven days on the train in between stops. Seven days is a long time for someone who likes to adventure and live life to the full. The stops were good: the Kremlin Armoury in Red Square; a boat trip on Lake Baikal - the biggest lake in the world; the Great Wall of China. Tick, tick, tick. All fascinating cultural heritage sites that I enjoyed, but I felt locked in. I knew this wasn't for me and needed to bust out.

At the Russia-Mongolia border we were held in our cabins by guards with guns preventing us from escaping, like prisoners in the old regime; this was too extreme and brought home to me how much I don't like being confined and constricted and how much I do like stepping away from the well-trodden paths. So in Ulaanbaatar I chose to get off the train for a few weeks and wander away from the tracks, the well-photographed and well-plied route. Robert Frost's "road less travelled" is an appealing road for me. I know that the main tourist attractions are attractions for a very good reason; they are worth seeing and photographing, but I become more fully present and engaged when I am in charge of my own destiny, exploring, discovering, adventuring and roaming the unbeaten paths.

If there is a narrow street in a city away from the Central Square, Main Street, hotels and shops, I will take it. I follow the white rabbit in my mind, and like Alice, I find myself in curiouser and curiouser lands, instinctively exploring the warrens of local communities and coming across charismatic locals as they go about their everyday lives. I like to discover, to play with the kids, join families for tea, share vodka with the elders and make the women laugh with my charades. This enriches me and I would like to think that I enrich them, without being patronising or disruptive. I try to go local and do what the locals do - I trust that they know best in their climate and country. I wash like them, sleep like them, eat their foods, drink their drinks, and use their wisdom, medicines and cures. I am a guest in their country, I respect their culture, I try to behave as they would wish me to, and I genuinely and instinctively trust their local knowledge. When I feel people recognise this in me and accept me as a temporary member of the tribe or family, this is when I truly delight in the warmth, hospitality and acceptance. In return I, the tall, white, alien Westerner, teach them some English, share my food, amuse the children, fix things or provide some basic first aid. I do my best and often at least make them laugh. They must think I'm a crazy giant from out of space sometimes and I feel like one when I am delivering a baby in the jungles of Borneo or drinking goat's milk in a ger in the Gobi Desert... but this stretching - this new clumsiness or naivety trying to live in their world - is part of the fun and joy of travelling.

So when we all got off the Trans-Siberian in Ulaanbaatar, I stayed off. I said goodbye to my bunk buddies and friends I had made on the train, and chose to go solo in Mongolia. The remaining passengers looked uncomfortable with my decision - what was I going to do, where was I going to go, where was I staying that night, had I booked a hotel? But I was happy, back in my element, away from the physical and mental confines of the metal boxes.

I loved Mongolia. My general love is for South East Asia: Kalimantan, Sumatra, Java, Malaysia, Cambodia, Papua, and Indonesia. I would describe myself as a "jungle bunny," in my most preferred element when I am almost claustrophobically hemmed in by natural rain forest and primary jungle; revelling in the steaminess, sweatiness, humidity, buzzing insects and stifling heat. Give me Borneo, the Amazon, West Papua any time and I'll have my shorts and boots on and a machete in my hand in a jiffy. However, Mongolia's open vastness and breath-taking panoramas captured my heart straight away, with its far-reaching open vistas, plains and plateaus, distant hazy hills and giant expanses of sky with occasional cumulus nimbus pierced by wheeling vultures and eagles. Magnificent. In the near distance, pastures are dotted with white tents or gers, and goats, sheep, camels and horses abound.

Rural Mongolia is like a land of make-believe where giant battles are fought, heroes gallop across the plains and dragons swoop down from the hills to grab sheep in their talons. A colossal stage steeped in centuries of drama; a place of Genghis Khan, Mongolian hordes, horses, condors, monasteries, invasions and bloodshed. Mongolia felt like an old and wise country, yet one willing to embrace the future. Solar panels on the traditional gers feed mobile phones and TVs and goatherds connect openly with other nations and talk positively about their future on the world stage.

I was delighted to be free again. On the very day I broke from the confines of packaged travel on rails, I was off in an indestructible Russian Nissan van with 16 Mongolians for a 17-hour, bone-rattling drive into the Gobi Desert. Yee hah! It was very rough going and quite unnerving at times as we tilted and rocked and ground our way over the rocks and floods. The drivers swapped after midnight, though they were both kept busy fixing the van or negotiating muddy tracks, pulling up five times to tighten the wheel nuts which had shaken loose! In the middle of the night we stopped for a comfort break. Ladies had to wander off and squat where we could. I took my head torch and when I threw the beam around out of curiosity, I saw a camel leg next to me while I was squatting and three camel skulls as I walked back to the van. I was tired from no sleep and now in the Gobi Desert, surrounded by sun-bleached skeletons, it all felt a bit surreal...

For the next week I had a wonderful time trekking in the Gobi Desert and living with the nomads in their gers. I felt very privileged to share their existence and they taught me how to manage the ger's ropes and canvas to adjust for the weather, cooking and sleeping. One night, sharing with Ari, a Mongolian teenager, a dust storm kicked off, banging and crashing all around us, shaking our ger and causing the heavy canvas to flap with great thumps. We couldn't sleep for the noise and got covered in sand which blew in through the vents. Ari didn't seem to care much so I got dressed and went outside twice into the storm, with sand and grit in my eyes, a howling gale, and a head torch, to tie the canvas down. I felt absolutely at ease at 0300 putting my local knowledge into practice. It was one of those special moments when the travelling, the customs, the immersion, come together and I could have a go at authentic Mongolian life and live it to the full.

Back in Ulaanbaatar I investigated rumours about some sort of record breaking horse festival out on the Steppe. I was certain there was a big event on from the chat out in the Gobi, but no one in the capital seemed to know about it, not even the tourist offices. I persevered in my pursuit of this tantalising rumour, knowing from travelling off the beaten track that listening to the locals is a great way to discover hidden adventures. After some persuasion and dispute, my hostel owner found a chauffeur who was passing where I thought the festival was and he agreed to drop me off; there was only one main road going west out of Ulaanbaatar so if something was out there, we would pass it.

I packed a light bag and joined two mature, Korean gentlemen in the back of their leather-seated, air-conditioned hire car. I think they were upset to share their luxury with such a scruffy backpacker and smiled condescendingly when I indicated I was getting dropped off en route. When we arrived in the middle of the Steppe where, as I expected, there were thousands of cars, gers and herds of native Mongolian horses, their faces were a picture. Clearly a spectacular event was about to happen that they were going to miss out on. I just got out of the car, grinned and waved goodbye. I knew that I was on the right trip. Life is an adventure, not always a chauffeured ride.

As the only Westerner I could see, I joined in for two days to watch two World Record attempts. On the first day over 11,125 Mongolians in national dress rode in the biggest horse parade on record. It went on for hours while we chanted ourselves raw and when they saw me among the Mongolian crowds, they laughed and waved. I could feel my heart pumping and spirits soaring, moved to witness such a magnificent event. The atmosphere was incredible; such a positive celebration of culture and tradition, in such an awesome setting. It was a truly extraordinary spectacle. On the second day, they broke the

World's Biggest Horse race record - an incredible 4,279 horses racing 27 kilometres across the Steppe.

This is why I travel. This, to me, is living life to the full. This goes to show what an amazing time we can have when we try the road less travelled, explore the unknown and discover that life is an adventure.

Chapter 7
Stretch

Stretching means leaning, extending, strengthening or unbending in order to reach something (like a goal). Stretching helps me to develop and grow, like exercising life muscles. The more I do, the more I know I can do. The more I achieve, the more confident and competent I become. But I have to step up and out of my comfort zone to do this. I give things a go; I try hard and once we do those two things, we are more amazing than we realise. Living in the stretch zone is living life to the full. The emotions and energies stimulated from stepping into the stretch zone are fundamental motivations for me. Feeling mentally, physically, spiritually and emotionally stretched; focused, motivated and alive.

Imagine for a moment sitting in your comfort zone, doing stuff that you are completely at ease with - answering emails, watching TV, going for a walk, hoovering, having a cuppa. Your feelings in the comfort zone may include being relaxed, comfortable, feeling safe, feeling in control, possibly boredom or complacency, perhaps pleasantness and calm. Your mind may be quiet or rather empty, potentially wandering distractively. You may be thinking of other things, planning, or using the time to think, processing or escaping from the humdrum. Your body will be quite relaxed; your energy levels low or flat. It is beneficial to be in the comfort zone; it is relaxing, de-stressing and recharges your batteries; giving you downtime and allowing you to "just be." However, if we stay in our comfort zone, we will learn less, be less capable and skilled, less wise and experienced, and the more stuck we will be in our safe, controlled place.

At the opposite end of the scale is the Panic Zone. Imagine now jumping out of a plane if you are scared of heights, giving a presentation to a thousand people if you hate giving presentations, or expecting a loved one to come home at 2200 and it is now the next day and there has been no communication. The panic zone is not a nice place to be. Here feelings may include anxiety, stress, worry, being scared, sick and tense. Your mind may freeze or dart about ineffectively not able to focus on one thing, or feel full of clamour and blood roaring. Your energy levels may be very elevated, but unsustainably hyperactive. Your physical state may be uptight and taut; perhaps you would be physically shaking, tense, white, sick or sweaty.

In between these two zones is the Stretch Zone. You are neither comfortable nor so rattled that you feel sick and out of control. You may be near the comfort zone or not far off your panic zone, but you are not actually in either one. You may still experience some worry and nervousness, but not so much that you can't cope and you feel ill with it. The positive side of this nervousness is that it carries feelings of anticipation, excitement, adrenaline and "buzz." You may feel *in the zone* or in the *flow*. Instead of negative stress there might be a positive stress called *eustress*, which helps you perform. Your mind is very sharp and focused here. You are switched on and quick witted. You may feel motivated or inspired, energised, engaged, active, on edge or "pumped." After the event, you are likely to have sensations of satisfaction, fulfilment, achievement or relief.

And you will have unlocked some of your potential, releasing innate talents and strengths, gaining confidence and competence, all of which usefully set you up to live life more fully in the future. Stretching stimulates a positive cycle of events; the more you stretch, the more you will be able to do. Your stretch zone will move outwards, your comfort zone will increase and your panic zone will reduce. Your life broadens and builds.

In the stretch zone I get to stretch my senses and abilities, stretch my knowledge, experiences and memories, and extend my situational awareness, intuition, emotional intelligence, resilience, competence and confidence, preferably keeping away from the panic zone which is unpleasant and retracting. The more I achieve, the more I realise I can achieve. Stretch is when high challenge meets medium to high ability. This is where the magic happens and the flow takes over. Low challenge combined with medium or high ability is underwhelming and can induce complacence or boredom. High challenge with low ability is a step too far into the panic zone, and can create stress, anxiety, tension and fear.

A stretch is a challenge, but it is an enlightening place where you learn, develop and grow. I like it here. Feeling the stretch is another reason why I step up and challenge myself to live life to the full. I feel more alive in this place and fully present. I love learning and growing. I enjoy being challenged - even when it is dangerous, uncomfortable or scary. I get a perverse pleasure when I have to dig deep for more energy or courage, be gritty, determined, tough and resilient. I start to spark and this ignition, this buzz, this alertness, this positive, physical energy is what I seek and thrive upon. It shines most brightly in the challenging places where I believe there is deep and meaningful living.

This perverse pleasure, or contradictory enjoyment of difficulty and danger, is fascinatedly explored in *Mountains of the Mind*, which examines the psychology of why people risk their lives to climb mountains. The author Robert Macfarlane, himself a mountaineer, describes the tantalising juggling or "agitation" between hope and fear, danger and safety, and life and death. It is when one is near to death that one feels most alive, that this extreme risk is "central to the experience." Many explorers - such as Scott or Mallory - risked and lost their lives in the pursuit of either the challenge itself or the feeling it spawns of living on the brink where life and death are in a fine balance. I would define this as the "edge," the unstable margin between high stretch and panic.

I think the edge is where we dare to go, until we pull back. The edge, at its most dangerous and sharpest, is where life and death hang in a balance. A delicate thread links the two at the breaking point, subject to the forces of a breathless teetering; a vital battle. Many have fallen either side of the edge in their pursuit of it. Mallory, Irvine, Scott, Oates, Wilson, Bowers and Evans famously battled and lost, falling on the wrong side at the bitter and painful end. Shackleton and his crew, Amundsen, Hillary and Tenzing Norgay famously battled and won.

The edge can be addictive, an obsession too. It can lure people towards it again and again. George Mallory in *Climbing Everest* talks about the "sheer joy" found at the edge, where man chooses to go and meet the challenge of the mountain in a struggle for life itself. Mallory attempted to climb Everest three times, dying on the third attempt, *"...for the spirit of adventure to keep alive the soul of man."* The edge can be like a drug. It gives off a high - especially afterwards - and leaves you wanting more. I don't think I am addicted to it, but I do go and seek it occasionally in my quest to live life to the full. This is at the sharp end of my list, where I purposefully and committedly put myself into an extreme and dangerous environment to test and challenge myself.

The edge is where life's electricity can be felt, where energy crackles and sparks; when we feel most vibrant and vital. It is where heart-felt fear and danger live; when near to death one feels most alive. Experiencing the vitality of the edge is one reason why we climb mountains, seek adventures, explore the unknown and set off on expeditions, because it is at the edge where emotions, experiences and memories amplify and intensify. I don't necessarily enjoy it at the time, but I do feel tremendously animate, energised and alert. I am very present, living richly in the moment. **I am deeply experiencing the fantastic and the terrible, and within the terrible, there is often the fantastic**. The edge is a significant place. It is remarkable and consequential; it brands you and lives on in your dreams for years.

I still get scared. I still get anxious and nervous. Many people think I don't have fear, but I do, I am human, it's just about how I manage it. One lady who was creating an exhibition on fearless women from around the world asked me two questions:

What fears did you have before and during the expedition to the South Pole?

I had many fears – deep and superficial, life-threatening and inconsequential, including:

– Death!
– Life-threatening injury
– Frostbite / losing fingers, etc.
– Polar Thigh
– Having an accident
– Crevasses
– Not making it to the South Pole
– Not even being able to start
– "Polar shock" (being unnerved by the surreal and extreme conditions)
– Quitting
– Going to the toilet
– Not being strong enough or fit enough
– Eating
– Losing too much weight
– Being unable to pull the 80kg pulk uphill, into the wind, for 1000km
– Going uphill (I hate going uphill)
– The cold (-20 down to -40 + wind chill)
– Crying

- Looking a fool
- Being rubbish
- Being worse than the others
- Not getting on with the guide or the others
- Being too slow
- Losing or breaking the tent, skis or other critical equipment / setting the tent on fire whilst cooking
- Falling over
- Not being able to ski
- The sastrugi
- The weather
- Too much wind or snow
- Not being able to sleep
- 24-hour daylight and its psychological impact

There are 31 fears on that list and probably many you will recognise. There were tangible fears and psychological ones, embarrassing ones (like going to the toilet) and vulnerable ones (like being worse than the others); typical human fears. Her second question was:

How did you overcome them?

This is where the cool stuff sits. I have accumulated many coping mechanisms, strategies and tactics from past experience, including mantras and reference points from when I have succeeded. It's about resilience. It's about positive psychology, having positive thoughts (negative thoughts made me lose energy) and mental toughness. This is what I believe in and what I speak passionately about. Here are some of my beliefs and mantras for coping psychologically:

- Feel the fear and do it anyway / **embrace the fear**
- I can. "This girl can"
- The Stretch Zone is the best place to be
- Live life to the full
- Attitude is 95% of the challenge / solution and you can always...
- **Choose your Attitude** (this was printed on one of my skis)

- **Pain is temporary, Pride is forever** (this was printed on the other ski)
- **Dig Deep**
- **Step Up, Don't Give Up**
- Listen to your **Don't Quit Tigers**, not your Give-Up Gremlins
- "Don't Quit" poem, "If" and "Desiderata"
- Churchill – "**When you're in hell, keep going**"
- **Role Model the Way**
- I have survived worse
- **What doesn't kill you, makes you stronger**
- If they can do it, I can do it (When I was at my worst, I thought of our guys and girls in war zones, coping with trauma and IEDs)
- "Grrrrrr!" (gritting teeth, screwing up the courage)
- Naming things to soften their power over me i.e. all my folders were labelled "Sarf Pole" just to make me chill about it

And then here are some of my more pragmatic solutions which helped me overcome fears by making me more physically ready for the edge:

- One year of preparation - the more prepared, the more confident I was in my own capability
- Physical training - aerobic, core stability, strength and lots of tyre pulling - 700 miles pulling two tyres along the beach
- Polar training in Norway twice, including crossing the Hardangervidda for 100 miles
- Reading books to understand the challenge, mentally prepare and know what to expect
- Talking to experts and polar travellers for those tips that only people who have done it really know
- Hardening my feet (I walked a lot in bare feet!)
- Pumped up music
- Vodka!

There are many, many coping strategies and tactics here and so much of it is psychological; attitude is king and queen on these occasions. There are also pragmatic and high performance behaviours in the training and physical preparation. But the point here is "you can." A stretch is a stretch but not an impossibility.

If I specialised in one discipline, I would be much more competent and confident, but I force myself to take on very different challenges in very different climates requiring very different skill sets and qualities. This stretches me each time as I find myself facing fresh events or activities that I have never done before, which cuts me back down to amateur level competency and naïve immaturity. I get nervous all over again as I face the fresh challenges, new technical knowledge and unknowns ahead. Many adventurers or sportspeople focus on one, maybe two disciplines or perhaps participate in triathlons which involves three disparate pursuits. They get more skilled, knowledgeable and proficient; in fact, the wisdom suggests that it takes 10,000 hours of practice to master something. I flit from one discipline to another, from mountaineering, to sailing, to trekking, to skiing cross-country, to flying, to horse-riding, with a steep learning curve each time. My mental, physical and technical toolbox has to be built up each time to become relevant and suitable, which is partly what pushes me and gives me my stretch, but it's not a comfortable transition from one to another.

My "technical cupboard" looks like Mr Ben's changing room from the old TV series; my home is like an adventure showroom housing ice-axes, paddles, skis, bows and arrows, "foulies" (yacht wet weather clothing), fancy dress outfits, ropes, crampons, thermals, thermoses and a sequined Union Jack mini-dress (South Pole attire, of course)!

Although I own a lot of different kit, I normally travel light: 5 kilograms in a 15-litre rucksack for a month. So when I took up winter mountaineering (stretch zone) with the aim to summit Everest (the edge), I was a bit taken aback when my instructor went through the kit I would need. Guess how many different items you need to go winter mountaineering in the Alps? Sixty-four! A dream for a techy gadget-lover but also confusing and expensive - how was I supposed to climb a mountain with so much to carry? This was the first indication that winter mountaineering was going to stretch me; then there are the four most critical things you do need to "pack" if you are to survive:

- Mental toughness
- Technical knowledge
- Acclimatisation
- Physical fitness – especially cardiovascular

My first winter mountaineering trip, Step One preparation for the Big One was on Ben Nevis in February - Britain's highest mountain standing at a very modest 1343 metres compared to Everest's 8848 metres. It was my first stab at mountaineering and I was nervous and felt unprepared. I wrote in my diary before I left:

> *More compass lessons this morning in bed with Alex! Getting rather nervous about going on Sunday and not being fit enough, young enough and experienced enough for next week. I am going into this on my own, with no climbing expertise at all, confused about how to use a compass, without any kit, and having not been to the gym enough. And I bet I'm with a load of 20-year-old hill walkers! Snow-holing overnight sounds interesting though...*

The day before I left, I went out to pick up a couple of orange "Survivor Bags," then back to my flat to pack and get my head round what I was about to do. It was difficult to think straight with parents, step children, kittens, boyfriend and sister all demanding brain space. Dad was due in hospital, Mum was worried about the expedition and sister was separating from her husband. My new kitchen was halfway through completion and nothing was where it should be. It must have been about 2330 when I finally crashed out to sleep on the sofa with the kittens. Why the sofa? Because the first Grand Prix of the season was due to start at 0330! I half slept and half watched Lewis Hamilton win, and got up at 0800 for eleven hours of travelling up to Ben Nevis via tube, train, bus, flight and finally a coach to the Onich Hotel near Fort William.

With trepidation I went down to dinner to meet the rest of the guys - and as I feared, they were all fit men, much younger than me, and with a fair amount of mountain and climbing experience. Bother! Why couldn't there have been one girl or someone completely unfit and inexperienced?! Oh yes, that was me. On the morning of Day One I packed and dressed as best as I could, not knowing quite what to do, what to wear or how to wear it and went down to breakfast with an empty and jangling stomach. After breakfast we had a session to go through our "essential kit;" we were advised to leave everything else behind and consider the weight of everything we took in order to travel FAST and LIGHT. I wasn't feeling either fast or light. I was feeling encumbered, inexperienced and generally unfit in body and mind. A standard one day's kit included head torch and spare batteries, map, compass, thermos flask of tea, litre bottle of water, thin thermal gloves, thick leather gloves, mitts, harness, helmet, crampons, ice axe, ski poles, whistle, survival bag, packed lunch, spare fleece / jacket, waterproof jacket, waterproof trousers, sunglasses, goggles, sun cream, money and tissues. And there was I hoping to just take some cheese sandwiches and a KitKat.

So I had to learn to climb up a mountain whilst carrying a rucksack full of gear... and that was without technical kit such as rope, carabiners, belay devices, etc., which were being carried by our guide. We drove to Aonach Mor and had the luxury of catching the gondola up to the snow line, where there was a ski resort in full swing. I felt quite jealous and resentful of the holidaymakers skiing about rucksack-free.

Once on the snow we spent the day learning snow and ice skills: how to walk up steep slopes in crampons either digging in the two toe spikes or travelling with one foot sideways and flat and one foot pointed into the snow (third position in ballet); walking down steep slopes - heels in; traversing - using as many points as possible and cutting an edge; and moving over bare rocks in crampons - not my favourite as there is nothing to dig into for purchase. We learned how to use ice axes (the pick, the shaft and the adze), how to cut steps and how to hold and carry the axe correctly (uphill hand, adze forwards). We practiced self-arrest when falling down a mountain slope: flipping onto our front, using the ice axe with the adze into the shoulder and digging the pick into the snow to slow down. We created a slippery run which we practiced on several times each, going down on our bottoms and stopping to the right and left, going down head first on our backs and going down feet first on our fronts. We tended to slide a further two metres before stopping - and that was on a relatively gentle slope on soft snow - making me worry about what it would be like when we were on a steeper gradient. We practiced making bucket seats - deep seats in the slope using the adze end of our ice axes.

We also went walking to put some skills into practice and look at different types of snow and ice formations, such as the rather beautiful hard rime that freezes on the windward side of structures. It was all pretty tiring, though, and that was the EASY day! Back at the hotel, totally wiped out, I had to unpack my entire rucksack and put the wet stuff into the drying room. I showered and crashed for a while, ate dinner and then crashed again for the night with twitching legs as I tried to sleep with dreams of falling.

The next day, according to my diary, was one of *"THE toughest days of my life I think."* We drove to Bidean nam Bian to the south of Glen Coe and, without the luxury of a gondola, had to walk in to the mountain for two hours, climbing 600 metres which almost killed me. Then we walked a further 200 metres with crampons in thick snow, which also almost killed me. It was slow, hard going. I slogged and slogged with shaking legs, one step at a time. By the time we got to the bottom of a gully - our main destination - I was done for. I have always felt especially challenged going upwards and with three hours climbing, little mountain fitness and blisters on my heels in my new, inflexible Millet boots, I was struggling.

Paula Reid

However, the worst was over and the rest of the day was interesting and enjoyable technical training before coming back down. We spent three hours learning how to belay and belaying each other up the 200 metre gully. This involved digging a bucket seat in the snow, burying an ice axe above it, clove hitching a sling to it, carabinering a rope to the sling with another clove hitch, tying the other end to the harness with a double figure of eight and then sitting in a snow bucket seat ready to belay someone up a 30 metre length of rope. I body belayed at first, with the rope around my body and over my arm. Then I used a belay device, and then a stomper belay - which is where you bury your ice axe deep in the snow and stand on it with the rope through that. Learning all these new technical skills was, for me, upper stretch zone. Big time.

While I sat in my snow bucket with my helmet on and my rucksack beside me, knowing that someone (Martin) was depending on me keeping him safe, lumps of snow and ice fell on my helmet from above where the other three were climbing. I had an amazing view but got very, very cold. Fingers, feet and bum all went numb eventually. Martin climbed up the 30 metre length of rope and once he was safe, shouted down to me to release the belay. With frozen fingers I then had to pull my ice axe out of the snow, undo the knots and re-clip the sling and carabiners to me, put my rucksack on and climb up on my own! It was pretty vertical and icy and hard work with my exhausted and shaking legs. I had to hammer in the ice axe, and then move each foot just using the toe spikes; ice axe in, one foot up toes only, other foot up toes only, ice axe in, etc. It didn't feel that the toe spikes were enough to hold me in to the icy wall and I must admit I relied on my belay rope for extra support - which you are not meant to do.

When I got to where Martin was sitting, my energy was spent and I naively thought it was my turn to sit down... But no, I had to climb up again, leapfrogging him another 30 metres! Once there I immediately had to set to work to secure myself and belay him up to me. Slow work and freezing when you are not doing anything much physically but sitting in a hole made of snow and belaying. It was also quite windy in the gully so it was hard to hear and work out what was going on. This was all the more difficult for me as I didn't know what was likely to be happening or what the typical jargon was. As on the boat, I felt huge pressure from lack of experience and specialist language while people were depending on me. It took us three hours to go up that gully.

My stretch zone had gone from gentle stretch to bordering-on-panic and it gave me all those wonderful things that come with it: focus, exhilaration, adrenaline, personal growth, satisfaction, and elation.

We then had to get all the way down again which meant literally stepping off the edge of the mountain, leaning back, digging in heels and striding steeply downhill in the snow. This was tiring, potentially dangerous if you slipped and definitely scary if you don't like heights, but I loved it: marching confidently down a mountain in virgin snow with a great view. The effort was worth it and the contrast between the very stretchy bits when I was scared and exhausted made the striding downhill all the more rewarding. It was that bitter-sweet juxtaposition between hellish endurance and heavenly delight. Winter mountaineering was a snowy white drug and I was hooked.

I was the fastest down and feeling really confident. I was in flow and in my comfort zone, totally unfazed by the vertical descent that the others were nervously confronting. We all have our strengths and weaknesses, and I suddenly felt buoyant and talented again, in contrast to my 20-year-old male mountain-goat partners. We took our crampons off at the snow line and trekked down the 600 metre path with pain exploding in each knee cap as we took giant strides down the rocky way. It had been a tough, tough day. At the end I was physically tired all over, blistered on toes and heels, with throbbing knees, aching legs and a dehydration headache. But I had also loved it in a funny, brutal way and the experience wasn't over yet.

The next morning I hobbled stiffly down to breakfast with calves and thighs, toes and heels, crying out in agony. How was I going to survive the day if I couldn't even manage one set of carpeted hotel stairs? The challenge for today - on already shot legs - was to go to Ben Nevis and do the Carn Mor Dearg (CMD) arête - or "ridge." How, I had no idea. When we got up to the Charles Inglis Clark Memorial hut, I had a very windy pee off the parapet and put more blister plasters on with gaffer tape. The worst bit was then trekking up and up and up in deep snow. I trudged, swore, shook, stopped and panted. Several times I thought I wasn't going to be able to go another step. Mind over matter. **One step at a time**. Gritted teeth.

An especially steep bit at the end was a killer, but luckily another guide joined us and he paced it out in short steps for me to follow: head down, two steps, stop, catch breath, two steps, stop, catch breath... Eventually we got to the top. "Piece of cake!" I exclaimed as I collapsed face down in the snow at the top in a comedy turn. Even in dire straits there is always a place for humour. The others, who were all sitting calmly drinking tea, laughed. They had been waiting for me and watching my gargantuan struggle up the hill, but I redeemed myself with my new catchphrase and "Piece of Cake" became a team motto.

We trekked along the one-metre-wide ridge for about two hours, roped up in pairs and walking either side of the ridge counter-balancing each other, so if one slipped in theory the other person's body weight would stop them from falling down the mountain. I was totally OK with this, once again back in my comfort zone while others were in their stretch zone bordering on panic; we are all different. I could now support and encourage the rest of the team who were nervous walking so close to the edge. Unfortunately for me, but perhaps not for them, it was cloudy so we didn't have great views, but knowing that the mountain dropped steeply down either side of us was thrilling. It began to snow with a harsh easterly wind and one side of my face iced up with fernlike patterns up my cheek. Everyone said it looked very cool.

After grabbing a quick bite of lunch, sheltering behind a rock from the wind, we then strode down again like the day before: a steep descent in virgin snow, one metre deep. I was fast and elegant going down, keeping up with the two guides and gabbling enthusiastically away, every now and again tapping each boot with my ice axe to get rid of the balling snow which makes your boots slippery. At one point I was walking in front of the two guides and they threw a snowball which rather unexpectedly and accurately hit my head, enough to unbalance me. I went into a steep fall and had to do a heroic ice axe arrest which was good to practice in reality! I think it gave the guides a heart attack but I was laughing all the way, pleased and exhilarated that my training had kicked in.

Back at the hotel I collapsed on my bed, aching, my feet hurting; I had a headache, was really dehydrated and physically tired all over, and coughing constantly. I decided not to go out the next day and allow my body to recuperate. I did some stretches, drank lots and lots of water, went for a short walk and slept a lot. It made my last day so much better, as I wrote in my diary:

I actually quite enjoyed 95% of today. Blimey. I felt lively and muscled and strong again. SO glad I took a day off. As it was, the other four guys were quite done in, and one even returned to the car to sit it out.

We returned to Aonach Mor to traverse the Douglas Boulder (West to East). I set off first with Chris [the guide] and we beat a swift start with the others far behind – it felt good to be in the front for a change, rather than way behind. Weather very bad today with strong winds gusting to 40 mph, knocking me physically sideways a few times – I wouldn't like to be on top of a ridge when that happens.

Walked on to the Douglas Boulder. A narrow gully with wind howling through it. Andy and I belayed each other up it for a couple of hours. I enjoyed it. And then we got to the top which was amazing (and I guess, always will be, even in a white out) and then we ABSEILED down. Something I'd always wanted to do. Felt weird leaning back with just rope holding you and my mind was telling me it was wrong at first, but once you do your first bounce down, it's great fun!

And then the three of us (Andy, me, Mark) walked all the way down, sometimes in snow up to our waists, crampons off and back to the car. Felt so much better having had a good day on the hill. Felt very worthy and satisfied and proud. Great dinner, lots of G&T's.

I had been fully in my stretch zone for the whole course, occasionally bordering on panic, and many times I had felt discomfort, fear and uncertainty. Each time I had to step up. Step up to the challenge and push myself mentally and physically onwards and upwards. At the time, the effort was very demanding, sometimes painful, often torturous, but usually grimly satisfying, and afterwards, or during the times that I felt confident, I experienced extreme elation, a high of adrenaline and an immense satisfaction with life. This is living life deeply, richly and fully, embracing both the tough stuff and the great stuff equally. I had hated and loved the winter mountaineering, but at least it made me feel fully alive, exultantly discovering my own deep valleys and peaks.

Four months later Alex and I flew to Aberdeen and spent our three-year anniversary in the sleet, hail and snow of Scotland in June, climbing Munro Lochnagar, 1150 metres. Then on Saturday 21 June it was D-Day for the Alps. I had booked, again in preparation for Everest, an "Introduction to Alpine Mountaineering" course. I was gradually stepping up my altitudes and getting as much wintry, technical experience as I could.

Arriving in Chamonix - where according to statistics, one person dies every day in a summer climbing season - I once more felt out of my depth. There were so many potential disasters waiting to befall me, and I was so inexperienced. Stretch zone. Big time. Nerves had knotted my stomach and my throat was dry. We had a team meeting scheduled in the hotel at 0830 and I was hoping for a big, friendly group in which I could hide and impress people with my banter. I imagined a nice guide, smiling and forgiving, and a climbing partner who was slow, unfit or perhaps overweight, hopefully with very little experience…

The worst case scenario walked in. Just two people: the guide, a wee Scottish man, aged 50 and looking weathered and very experienced, and the only other client, John, 6' 3", no fat, a sniper fresh from Iraq, training for Everest, and who'd been in the gym doing three-hour sessions on the step machine with a heavy rucksack and his boots on… Damn! It couldn't have been much worse. And how often is a girl disappointed to be spending the next week tied to a fit sniper up in the Alps?! I started apologising and making excuses straight away - how little experience I had, how unfit I was, how I had only in the last four months taken up mountaineering, and yes, I was aiming to do Everest. I must have been a guide's worst nightmare. Still, I had a good attitude, which counts for a lot out on those damn hills.

You know you're in the Stretch Zone when you can't even pee successfully. On day two, I had to practice using my new she-wee while roped up within ten metres of the two guys. The first time I didn't quite get the position right and ended up with wet pants, which isn't ideal when mountaineering for five days. There was a lovely moment though when my two travelling companions asked me solicitously how I had got on - a Scottish pro-climber and a sniper from Iraq wondering how my first day with a fake penis went. There are so many moments of hysteria on these occasions where basic everyday tasks collide with extreme survival situations. The contrast is so surreal, and the pressure so great, that the hysteria provides a release. I told them that it had been a minor disaster. The second time, still roped up with the two guys turning their backs for me, I got the position right but made the fundamental beginner's error of peeing up against a rock face, getting splash back all over my one pair of climbing trousers. They laughed and taught me the basics of peeing standing up on a mountainside.

Then came the crevasse rescue training. We decided to travel with "Sniper John" in front, so he could do a lot of the hard work making tracks in the snow, with myself roped in the middle, being the least experienced, and our guide at the back so that if John did full down a crevasse, at least the guide was still available to technically aid with the rescue. We found an open crevasse and our guide very slowly and carefully talked us through the rescue techniques which were quite complicated to my inexperienced mind. He then suggested we attempt a rescue as if John had fallen down the crevasse. The guide unclipped himself from our ropes, and said, "Paula, you have a go at rescuing..." and before he had even finished his sentence, 6' 3" John had run and leapt off the edge into the crevasse, shouting "Yee hah!'" tied only to little, inexperienced Paula.

Luckily for him, and to the great relief of our guide, the tough, resilient, no-nonsense Paula kicked in. (I can do it when I have to).

Beneath the nerves and shaky banter, lack of fitness and training, a hard core of capability and crisis management is there inside. I dropped to the ground, twisted onto my front, remembered to lift my feet up (you can break a leg if your crampon-clad boots get caught in the snow) and stuck my ice axe into the snow for all I was worth. Shooting towards the crevasse like a rocket on ice (if there had been more friction, I am sure I would have left a trail of fire in the snow) I dug deep and dug in; my progress towards the edge slowed and I came to a grinding stop just in time. John must have dropped down quite considerably, which, knowing him, he doubtless enjoyed. He probably should have stayed down there too as he got the biggest rollicking from the guide that the wee Scott had ever given a client. John looked sheepish and apologised to me afterwards, but the truth was that I enjoyed the thrill of the very real challenge and it bonded us; showing them that I had an inner steel and as I laughed afterwards, I realised that I could do this. Once more, the stretch zone had bequeathed me with a confidence I didn't know I had, and gifted me with a crazy learning and laughter moment.

That night we stayed in another hut, but I slept badly surrounded by 23 male French mountaineers all snoring and farting. To cap it all, I had diarrhoea in the morning, which wasn't a pleasant experience in the mountain hut facilities. We climbed all day in metre deep snow. The following day we were up at 0450, breakfasted at 0500 and set off in the dark for a roped up trek across a glacier, then a traverse, then up a steep slope over the top into Switzerland, another slope and a final two tough hours in poor snow to the Talefre Hut standing at 3100 metres in a beautiful sunset.

However, in spite of the stretch and loving it, this was the day I made the decision not to do Everest.

You can't responsibly just go and do Everest. The agency which I had booked the Scottish winter mountaineering and the introduction to alpine mountaineering with had laid out a training regime for me. You have to know your stuff, technically, physically, mentally, and have to be acclimatised by steadily working your way up the altitude ladder, climbing a mountain that was 1000–2000 metres higher each time. So far, I was still on the nursery slopes; the big ones were all due to come over the following 18 months if I really put the hours and effort in. I was on the edge of my stretch-panic zone with my training so far, half-loving and half-hating the mountaineering as I oscillated between the two.

Sitting on a mountain peak at sunset after a hard day, of course I was loving it. I felt thrilled to be alive; I was living life to the full. I was bursting with energy, pride, exhilaration, and a love of life. I was physically and metaphorically on top of the world. I was in that peak state which comes so rarely in ordinary life; absolutely thrumming with positive vitality and dynamism. I had never felt so alive! Fresh, invigorated, capacious, abounding, sharp, confident, and capable.

But when I was struggling on the edge of my ability, ascending a vertical wall of icy rock with shaking legs, a sick stomach and desperately trying to work out what to do technically, feeling incapable, out of depth, weak and stupid, then I was not enjoying it at all. I was in my panic zone which is not such a fun place to be. No happiness during or after the event. Just fear.

These things are meant to be challenging. The famously bigger, harder ones - Everest, South Pole, North Pole, swimming the channel, rowing the Atlantic, sailing around the world - require you to dig very, very deep.

I wasn't a quitter, so a lack of enjoyment, and a feeling of inadequacy wasn't going to make me give up on Everest. However, having read quite a few books about climbing Everest, and spoken to lots of experts, guides and mountaineers, the shine of the challenge was wearing thin. The more people I spoke to about it, the less I wanted to do it. The Alpine technical mountaineers, including my guide, looked down at Everest. It wasn't a technical climb; it did not really need technical know-how. Out of all the people who go there to attempt the summit, only a third actually attempt the summit and out of those, statistically one in ten die which is why the last push in the "death zone" is so crucial. These weren't good odds. There were stories of clients determined to push on despite the weather, or their health, or their guide's advice. There are queues on the Hillary step. There is litter. There are Sherpas risking their lives for the paying clients. There are too many disasters and deaths.

As I stood on Mont Blanc that afternoon, with a stunning view across the mountain tops of France and Switzerland, my head cleared and enabled me to contemplate the bigger picture. I realised that I was only really attempting Everest so that I could tell people, "I have climbed Everest." It wasn't appealing to me in itself. I was doing it for a tick on my list and a bit of glory. The passion for the climb wasn't really there. I made a great decision then. Despite my drive for achievement, despite my list of things to do before I die, despite my investment already financially and personally, despite my "don't quit" mentally, and with tears running down my face, I decided not to do Everest. It was the right decision. I was happy with that, but it was also an emotionally charged one that had my soul grieving, my heart deflating and my stomach in knots.

I had a fabulous last day on the mountain, almost as if it were trying to lure me back from my decision. We were off at 0600 for a decent paced trek back across the Argentière Glacier. It was the most gently beautiful morning, the Alps in sun-rising glory, understated and soft. We travelled down a steep slope - me in my element again and happy knowing this was my last day - then traversed a gentler slope across the rocks, finishing with a pacey romp down a beautiful Alpine path and the luxury of a chair lift to Argentière.

That night Sniper John and I got drunk on quality French red wine in the clear air of Chamonix, surrounded by glaciers and Alpine life. We were both feeling fresh and exultant after our climb experiencing the pleasant after-glow of a job well done. Fresh air, exercise, amazing company, red wine, glaciers... my personal mountain climbed and behind me. Aiming for Everest had given me a brilliant collection of mountaineering experiences. I had climbed to the edge and chosen to pull back and I had aimed for the stars and landed on the moon. I felt stretched; victorious and euphoric.

Paula Reid

Chapter 8
Don't Quit Tigers

In a year of disaster and pain - my annus horribilis - I suffered three major traumas. I was rather unlucky to have three quite monumentally disastrous events happen to me within six months, but I don't regret that year. Life is messy, life can be challenging, but life is a journey. I don't wish for things not to happen; if you enjoy the rainbows, you have to put up with the rain. I learned a lot that year; my life enriched from the hardships, soul searching and pain, and I accomplished different achievements - more mental triumphs than physical ones. After all, it's not about the cards you're dealt, but how you play the hand. In other words, **pain is temporary, pride is forever** and **choose your attitude**. Throughout this terrible year, I clung to these two beliefs, and they helped me to not quit, despite the fact that my world was falling apart around me.

It started with one of those deeply gut-kicking "it will never happen to me" experiences. I found out that the man I was living with had been having an affair for the last two years.

A best friend was getting married in Scotland in January and I was due to be "Master" of Ceremonies. The main party of us, the bridesmaids and ushers, me and my other half, were in a minibus travelling from Inverness airport to the castle where we were all staying; it was snowing, the scenery was spell-binding and I was anticipating a romantic and stunning weekend. But it was stunning in a whole different way. On the minibus I received an email from a stranger. She explained who she was, what had been happening and gave me evidence. I experienced that deeply felt "whoomph" as the bottom of my world fell out. I couldn't breathe, my chest tightened, my senses shut down, and I imploded.

After a short while, when the internal explosion had abated and I was reeling in the aftershock, I slowly came round. It felt like I had passed out. I was still on the minibus, staring out of the window, but I felt much older and as if a long time had passed. When my senses began to kick in, I determined then and there to behave with dignity and respect. I'm not sure where this flash of clarity came from, but I think a strong influence was that we were on our way to a wedding, and the etiquette and manners of the occasion had inspired me. Looking out at the snowy landscape was also soothing and possibly softened my instinctive reaction. I felt a calm resolve take over and I made an agreement with myself that I was not going to make a scene, shout or scream and make a fool of him or me. So despite the raging pain, noise, anger and despair I felt, I also began to feel in some sort of control, which was weird, but very welcome. I am still impressed to this day that my head and heart decided to take this route and that I behaved decently and with dignity. We had plenty of emotions flowing but I didn't say or do anything major that I regret. I had chosen my attitude.

When we got to the wedding, I managed to smile at the bride-and-groom to be before extricating myself from the wedding party to find somewhere I could collapse in private. There then followed a most miserable time as myself and my partner faced each other with the news and then removed ourselves from the wedding. We tried our best to diplomatically disappear with little fuss and it was thanks to the mother of the groom for looking after me so well at this point. She brought me brandy as I was shivering outside in the snow, hiding from the other guests, and conveyed our apologies. What an occasion for this sort of revelation! We both travelled back to the airport in silence and tears, stayed in an airport hotel that night and then returned home. Months of misery followed. We split up and I was left living alone, in deep and overwhelming sadness. Strike one.

By April I was rallying and for the first time that year I decided to go out, do something active or sporty and meet new people. So I chose to play "no strings" badminton: just a turn up and play evening. This suited me as I was still feeling adrift and not predisposed to committing to anything long-term. I had been good at badminton once, playing every Friday night when I was growing up, but I hadn't played for years. Nervous at first, and not sure if I could rediscover my skills, I soon got back into it and the competitive instinct kicked in with a bit of showing off to be fair. In the second game I found myself in a cracking match with three very good players. The shots were fizzing off our rackets in impressive succession; drop shots, smashes, long over-arm shots; the pace was getting faster; the competitive edge sharper; and the effort, skill and determination were mercilessly rising.

But then there was a loud "CRACK!" and I abruptly stopped half-way through executing a long, overarm shot. I thought I had dropped my mobile phone on the wooden sprung floor which didn't make sense as I didn't have my phone on me. I was puzzled for a few moments and then felt extreme pain in my lower leg. After resting up for ten minutes and receiving a lot of embarrassing fuss from my new sporting partners, I tried to cycle home with just one foot on one pedal, which didn't really work. I was without my phone, in the dark, on my own, in the rain wearing badminton kit and trying to cycle. While I was pedalling abysmally on the pavement, a group of people walked out in front of me and I couldn't put my foot down to stop, so I fell off. As I lay on the wet pavement and they stared at me as if I were mad or drunk, I did feel quite sorry for myself. My attempt at going out, meeting new people and getting fit wasn't going too well.

When I finally got home, I put my foot up with a bag of frozen peas, and cried.

The next evening after work, I took myself off to the hospital and got the bad news that I had ruptured my Achilles tendon. I had been unlucky. I think that the tension of the affair over the last four months had taken a hold of me and I was more tight and brittle than usual; I honestly don't think I would have broken it if I had just spent those months relaxing, in love and having fun, moving and laughing. As it turns out, rupturing an Achilles tendon is one of the worst injuries you can endure. It is extremely painful, very debilitating and takes two years to recover from. Strike two.

For the next month I had a tough time. Anyone who has been on crutches will know that it's hard to cook, sweep the floor, take the rubbish out or carry a cup of tea when you are on crutches and live alone. In fact, most housework was quite impossible. My flat got dirtier and I got thinner. Luckily my sister lent me a trolley which I used to wheel my ready meal and drink along the hallway by hop-pushing it along with my hips, two cats watching either side for spillages. Fun and games.

It was physically hard work and awkward getting about, and less than a month later I was sitting at my desk in the home office typing, turned sideways to reach for my tea and my back completely seized up. I couldn't move; I couldn't even touch the top row of my keyboard. Nearly Disaster Three, but the situation was worse than I thought. Yes, I had temporarily put my back out, but what that then masked for the next few days was a large blood clot on my lungs - a rather dangerous Pulmonary Embolism was lying in wait which can be fatal. I thought it was my bad back that was hurting so much, but I later discovered that it was the blood clots pressing on my lungs. Apparently, if you have a leg in plaster, there is a likelihood of developing a PE. Blood from the injury or bruising doesn't get properly pumped around your body because you aren't using your leg muscles, and potentially builds into a clot which can then shift into your heart, lung or brain. The hospital where I was treated told me they were even considering putting patients with leg plasters proactively on Warfarin to avoid this.

Luckily at the time I had a friend staying with me as I couldn't get around on my crutches because my back was out! At 0500 one morning, after two nights of not sleeping because it hurt too much to lie down, I was in tremendous pain and desperately needed the toilet. I had held off for as long as I could, not wanting to wake my friend too early, but the situation was becoming pressing. He helped me out of bed and half-carried me (still in a plaster cast and on one leg) onto the toilet and then called an ambulance. At 0500 on a weekday morning, when you live quite near St George's Hospital, Tooting, it doesn't take long for a blue-light ambulance to come. I was still on the toilet when the paramedics entered my flat! After ECGs and an MRI, it was confirmed that I had several large blood clots on my left lung and I was then placed on Warfarin for six months. Disaster three had struck.

My annus horribilis story isn't about paddling the Mekong or skiing to the South Pole, but it is still about living life to the full, because living a full life means living a deep and rich life with its highs and lows and undulating, unpredictable narrative. It's about taking on all that fate deals us - the good hands and the bad hands - and the way you choose to play the cards you have been dealt. Inevitably life presents us with challenges and difficulties, pain and disaster, but more often than not these are temporary, passing chapters in our life stories. It is our choice of response to that pain which stays with us forever and that embodies resilience and growth. Pain is Temporary, Pride is Forever. I didn't give up or succumb to negativity.

For the two physical traumas I had to attend hospital twice a week for six months for my INR (blood) tests and participate in lung function tests, ECG and CT scans, and Biomechanics sessions, and to be honest, going to the hospital on my own for so many appointments, sitting in waiting rooms, and getting emotionally distressed from empathising with other patients' problems, got me down. However, I consciously recognised this creeping melancholy and managed to keep up a positive attitude with the hospital staff and patients, stuck to my physio and exercise regimes and generally preserved my work life without giving in to the malaise that was trying to take hold. I don't know for sure if I got depressed - I got quite teary very easily for a while - but I cracked on, focusing on what I had to do and kept busy. I welcomed the opportunity to slow down for a while. I have a tendency to live a fast paced and packed life, full of action and activity, targets and goals, but I recognised that it was good to have a period of quietude, a time to think and review my perspective. I also wrote my third book and watched a lot of the London 2012 Olympic Games which was obligingly inspirational and motivational. I was determined to get through and out the other side, and sure enough, I bounced back.

A few years later, that resilience kicked in again - during my training for the South Pole and during the actual expedition; **not quitting** was a very apposite attitude to have fostered.

* * *

As part of my South Pole training programme I chose to complete a well-known cross-country ski trail in Norway called the "Hardangervidda Crossing." The fact that the name starts with "hard" and "danger" perhaps should have told me something, and I completed the translation with the idea that "vida" (OK, different spelling) in Spanish means "life", so I named this Norwegian expedition the "hard danger life." The Hardangervidda itself is a National Park, a bit like the Lake District in the UK; a stunning scenic landscape of hills and lakes, which in wintertime becomes beautifully frozen and white. A trail around 120 kilometres long, marked by hazel branches called *kvisteruter*, dots the way over the hills and the lakes too. This was Amundsen's training ground for the South Pole.

The big challenge is to traverse the Hardangervidda on cross-country skis. Not many locals have done the entire crossing; they often complete a section on a weekend and stay in cabins on route, just carrying a day bag. The Norwegians ski as if born with them on, graceful, natural and efficient. We, on the other hand, were five amateur aliens determined to cross the whole of the Hardangervidda in one go, without having done much free-heel skiing before, pulling weighty pulks (carbon-fibre sledges) and camping on the ice each night. Stretch zone... one step at a time.

On the third day of our crossing, we happened to leap-frog a large group of Norwegians several times. They would proficiently ski past us then stop for a break while we humbly and doggedly skied back past them, feeling somewhat awkward and ragged in style. On the third passing, they asked our guide where we were from and what we were doing. When they heard it was our first time on cross-country skis and that we were tackling the whole Hardangervidda crossing, plus that I was doing it in training for the South Pole, their bemused expressions changed to something more akin to respect and admiration. They smiled and nodded at us and then organised themselves into a guard of honour, holding their ski sticks up in an archway for us to ski through as they cheered.

That felt good and got me watery-eyed because at this point I was suffering.

On the first morning of the Hardangervidda there is a steep hill that takes about two hours to summit. We had attached half-skins to the bottom of our skis which create a grip to stop us from sliding back down the inclines, but this hill was so steep it was easiest and best to take the skis off and climb up in our ski boots. My ski boots were prototypes and fresh out of the factory and unfortunately I was the one to discover a design fault. There was a hard ridge of rubber which protruded inside each boot around the heel area. As I clambered up the hill, pushing down hard for each upward step, the ridges dug in and scraped down my heels with every tread, inevitably rubbing the skin and flesh off each heel. This produced an area about 8cm^2 of raw, exposed flesh.

That night, as I heaved off my boots, lots of my heels came off with them. It wasn't pretty. Blisters are one of the most stupidly small yet painful things to get, especially on endurance challenges. They hurt way beyond their remit, ridiculously sore for their size and cause. I've had more traumatic and dramatic injuries that hurt less and grieve me less than a blister! And this was way beyond the blister category. Suffice to say that my heels hurt. A lot. And I still had eight days to go of free-heel skiing in the same damn boots.

However, I was determined to finish, and tried to concentrate on everything but the pain for the rest of the crossing. Medically we padded and bound my feet and I took painkillers, but I also had to devise various mental distraction techniques as I plodded along for another week. One step at a time, choose your attitude, pain is temporary, pride is forever, don't quit... As soon as we got to the end, the skis and boots came straight off and I sighed with relief and satisfaction. I'd done it. Not only had I completed the Hardangervidda Crossing, new on cross-country skis, pulling a pulk, camping each night on icy lakes and with two very raw heels, I had set myself a **positive reference point** for when I did the South Pole expedition. I could refer back to the training, the knowledge gained and lessons learned in every way, and know that I could persevere through pain and continue to ski. I had a successful anchor of achievement which I could then turn to when I was in trouble in Antarctica.

The further I push myself, the further I know I can push myself. The higher I reach, the higher I know I can reach. The deeper I have to dig, the more reserves I know I have within me next time.

When the going gets tough, how do you ever know whether to quit or not? When you are on a hard-hitting expedition or challenge, and if you have a choice, when might you justifiably give in? The Marathon des Sables - billed as the "toughest footrace on earth" - is one of the harder endurance challenges out there; an ultramarathon which gets tougher every year as the organisers turn the screws, essentially involving running 150 miles - or 5½ marathons - in the Sahara Desert over five days. This sort of challenge has "Pain is Temporary, Pride is Forever" written all over it; it's one that makes you suffer for the sake of the achievement, stretching competitors to push through the pain/heat/fatigue barriers and out the other side to the pride/success/triumph finish line. The website suggests that: *"No one can deny that finishing the MdS is an incredible accomplishment. But more importantly, you will walk away with a new slant on life - that you can achieve anything you set your mind to do."* Quite often, and quite understandably, competitors do not finish the Marathon de Sables. One competitor I know got very dehydrated, observed that many other runners were pulling up and receiving medical treatment, and also decided to stop.

But I know that he now regrets that.

On a somewhat lesser endurance event - the London to Brighton 54-mile bike ride - I was cycling it on my own one year, albeit surrounded by about 27,000 other competitors, and wearing a gladiator costume. I am usually very happy to wear a crazy costume on these days because it provokes me, the other competitors, the marshals and the spectators to smile and cheer, which makes for a happier and more interactive day. This feels great and coherent when it's sunny; however, when it is pouring with rain, the roads are flooded, and thunder and lightning are crashing and cracking all around, it's not so funny. Cyclists have their heads down, marshals are wrapped up in hoods and plastic ponchos and there aren't many spectators. The gladiator outfit now seems ridiculous, a poor choice of rainwear for an all-day challenge, and I'm getting drenched. My exposed legs are cold and my thick sheepskin boots are heavy and sodden.

My parents live exactly at the halfway point on the route, in a village called Copthorne, and my sister was visiting because it was Father's Day. They had a family conflab about how mad I was cycling in such ferocious weather. I must admit, it was pretty bad, but I was OK at this point; I was pumped up, battling on and insanely relishing the madness of the elements. In Copthorne, my sister kindly drove down to pick me up in her Range Rover and pulled me over: "Come back home. We've got a fire going and a nice hot stew and we're going to stay inside and watch a film this afternoon." At the time I wasn't tempted. Mentally I was feeling strong and determined. "No, thanks. I'm alright." I cycled on.

However, temptation had sowed its seed inside my head. There was now a different narrative. A switch. I was now cycling through floods of water in a ridiculous fancy dress costume, cold and soaked, to a backdrop of thunder and lightning, and now it felt much, much worse. It felt wrong and stupid to carry on. How funny that there were two completely conflicting perspectives. *Was it lunacy to carry on or resilience?* Was it derisible stupidity or admirable courage? Where I had been enjoying the madness, laughing crazily at the ridiculousness of my situation, bracing against the elements, feeling alive and electric, I now had a feeling of foolishness that I had turned down such a sensible suggestion. What was I doing? Seeing myself through my family's eyes I saw a lunatic. This and the lure of not having to cycle for another three hours in the storm, getting warm and dry, were too strong. I stopped half a mile later and turned for home.

I regret that. Yes, it made sense to stop, but where was my will? **If the will is there, then there is a way.** When you are in the thick of the storm, you have the choice to persevere, or as Churchill said: "When you are in Hell, keep going."

In many of life's challenges there are good, solid, sensible reasons to give up. But how do you know, at the time, and even afterwards, whether it was right to give up? Of course you are going to be suffering, that's why these challenges are tough, that is the nature of the beast. At some point, or at several points, you are going to feel exhausted, in pain, in difficulty and wanting to give up. But do you give up? In your head, a forgiving and beguiling voice will be saying to you: "Come on, that's enough now, you've given it your best shot. After all, every step is a victory, it's the journey not the destination that matters. You are in real trouble now so it's time to call it a day. You can't go on, it's sensible to stop, it's for your own good. Hey - look -

they've given up too." These voices are reasonable and appealing, but are they serving you right?

I call these the "give-up" gremlins and I try not to listen to them. Once they worm their way into your head, they are hard to dismiss. They are insidious and provocative. As soon as they sow their seeds of doubt and hope, an exit door begins to open in your mind, letting in the light and showing the way to a warm and welcoming sanctuary. A shining pathway appears in the gloom; an evacuation route materialises out of the darkness. It is at first vague and ephemeral, but becomes stronger and brighter the more you think about it and give it credible energy. It beckons more and more powerfully.

It is hard to resist the give-up gremlins. We all know about them. They are often described as the devil on our shoulder. They are our inner voices and they don't always have our best interest at heart. The fact is we have inputs - like someone saying something to us - which we then process through an internal filter, which then often distorts into a different message; frequently negative because we have interpreted, magnified or twisted it into our own dialogue. The inner voice misleads or misrepresents the actual facts. We apply our context and history and emotions, fears and needs.

The give-up gremlins are very persuasive, but giving up isn't always the solution. Giving up is easier, because it takes you *downhill*. I believe the solution is usually to **step up, not give up**. To rise to the challenge, dig deep. This uphill path, or this choice, is tougher, yet ends at a *higher finishing place*. A place of accomplishment, pride, fulfilment, confidence and resilience that will stay with you forever. What if you gave up just when the tide was about to turn? One more step, one more effort could have made all the difference. The end of the race is the time to stop, not before.

You are in it for the long run.

When the fun stops, the commitment starts. It is when we are at the hardest, darkest, steepest part of the journey that we most want to call it a day. But this is when you find your deepest, strongest, most incredible will power. When you have to dig deep, you will find there is more depth of resource within you. We are more capable than we think. There are reserves of energy and determination that lie buried within us, but they are there. They are there when we really need them, when it really matters. When we have a relatively easy life, we only scratch the surface; possibly down into the top 5% of our reserves. We are made of strong stuff, boys and girls, men and women. Not sugar and spice or snails and puppy dog tails, but resilience, fortitude, determination, hope, courage, grit and guts.

So what is your **point of reference**? When you are thinking of giving up, what do you think about? If you are thinking that it's OK to quit and of the times when you have quit before and taken the easy downhill path home, then that is what is going to be dominant in your head. The give-up gremlins will be whispering at you to quit again, playing with your mind. The tendrils of escape will twine around your thoughts and you will begin to construct a narrative which supports your exit to a kinder, warmer, and nicer place.

But if your point of reference is set at a higher bar, with higher standards, expectations and personal success criteria; if you think about all the times you HAVE coped, you have made it through, you have got to the finish without quitting, then this will dominate your head and feed your thoughts. Strong, tough, resilient, fierce. **The "DON'T QUIT" tigers.**

Chapter 9
Look Forward, Not Down

Look Forward, Not Down is about three key orientations in living life to the full; learning from the past, looking to the future and living in the present. Learning and growing from previous experiences and building that tool box, knowledge bank and resilience for future use. Being future focused and looking forward to living; aiming for where you want to be. And being fully present; mindful, living for the moment, seizing the day.

Look Forward, Not Down is also about being visionary; having goals, ambitions, aspirations and dreams; planning ahead and preparing thoroughly for the adventures to come, and keeping your head up; being alert and staying positive. Having goals gives us a sense of direction and purpose, looking to the future. The bigger, more aspirational and stretchy the goals, the more ambitious the dream or vision, the greater the preparation and planning. I have already written about many events in my life that I leapt into, almost with wild abandon or at least with very little preparation (just do it), but the big expeditions are planned and prepared to the greatest possible extent.

The goal or vision presents the target to aim for in the long term and focuses efforts and decisions strategically; the preparation provides the tactical detail. I have to keep looking forward to adjust my aim and maintain my motivation. If I look down, or become down-cast, I lose my way and the momentum.

This chapter is about all these elements and how they materialised and became tangible benefits during the preparation and commencement of my expedition skiing full distance to the South Pole.

In the aptly entitled *The Worst Journey in the World*, Apsley Cherry-Garrard, a surviving member of Scott's last expedition in Antarctica, claims that *"The man with the nerves goes farthest"* and though we are a nation of shopkeepers, who like to count the money and not the bravery or usefulness of such an expedition, those who sledge alongside *"will not be shopkeepers: [and] that is worth a great deal."* Those who sledge will not be short-sighted regulators, but far-sighted and visionary. Sledging to the South Pole is not about the money; it's about vision, ambition, purpose and, of course, living life to the full.

Before I skied to the South Pole, I thought it was impossible that someone like me would be able to achieve something that great. Famous bearded explorers had tried and failed, or only just achieved this and I was in awe of them; they were on a pedestal, elusive and famous, distant and eminent, men. The proposition was way off my scope.

I must admit that my list of "things to do" has a bit of a life of its own. I sometimes throw things onto the list without much thought, thinking they sound exciting and life-enhancing, but not always having the time at that moment in time to research or fully understand them. It's not until I go to do one, that I give it some consideration. I may have a conversation with someone who asks - "why haven't you done the Burning Man Festival yet?" And the Burning Man goes on the list as it seems like a good idea but I don't actually know what exactly it entails beyond a vague notion that it involves fire, bicycles and nakedness... Someone recently suggested doing the sardine run (not quite as dangerous as the bull run, but it does involve sharks!) and the pictures of it look amazing so it's on the list, but

I don't yet know what's involved or in which part of the world it happens. It will be one to look into in the future, when I feel like a diving trip or a watery experience. So, naturally, with a decent, full-bodied bucket list, "doing the South Pole or North Pole" ended up on it as a romantic concept.

Perhaps like many people I was mildly in love with the vision of the Arctic or Antarctica, seeing the polar bears or emperor penguins, but I wasn't actually contemplating an *expedition*. I thought that was beyond me as a normal, average, human being (limiting beliefs). It was only in 2013, the year following my annus horribilis, while I was still recovering from the ruptured Achilles, that I felt myself once more hankering "for a big one." It had been eight years since returning from the Global Challenge, and I wanted something hefty and challenging so I looked at my list.

My first thought was, "South Pole or North Pole, what's the difference?" So I called a friend called Jason De Carteret who had testicles and a beard and an "Ice-Truck" with 32 gears and six wheels, and who has skied both to the North and South Poles. He explained that essentially the North Pole was physical and the South Pole was mental. The Arctic in the North comprises sea-ice, not land, so the terrain is constantly moving and breaking, cracking and shifting, and it makes for a very interactive and dynamic environment to traverse. The North Pole expedition is extremely physical as skiers have to often stop and manoeuvre their pulk over and around great lumps of ice and sometimes the team have to chip in and help out. You can "ride" forwards, backwards or sideways from your destination because the ice flow is constantly moving like a travelator. I heard of one group who, while they were sleeping, drifted over the North Pole, so they achieved their aim without even realising it! The North Pole is the favourite of many expedition leaders because it's interesting, physically challenging and mentally stimulating. It also comprises polar bears and *wet* cold.

Antarctica, home to the South Pole, comprises penguins and dry cold. It is a flattish desert - drier than the Gobi. Antarctica is a land-mass so it doesn't shift like the Arctic, with a massive snow and ice-cap incredibly three kilometres thick in places. Much flatter than the Arctic but with great mountain ranges, such as Pensacola and Thiel, with glacial terrain. The South Pole challenge is more mental because you ski in a straight line, single file and crack on. There is not much to look at, not many physical challenges to break up the day, not much teamwork required, just the mental determination and resilience to keep going. The guides I talked to seemed to be recommending the North Pole, as it was more interesting and a lot cheaper, but I had a romantic hankering for the South Pole and Antarctica, maybe because it was so far away, or maybe because of its history.

Jason recommended that I speak with Helen, one of the few female polar guides, and her Norwegian company, Newland. We met in a rather dodgy pub in South London and hit it off. Helen loves life and loves her job. She is a tough cookie, with a permanent grin and no beard! She assured me that I could become a polar adventurer and introduced me to "Ski the Last Degree," an expedition where you get dropped at 89 degrees South and have to ski from there to 90 degrees. This takes a week to ten days including acclimatisation, covering a bit less distance and skiing a bit more conservatively in the first few days. I realised that "doing the South Pole" was do-able. But then Helen said, "Or you can ski full distance." Fatal. I then knew that Ski the Last Degree was not going to be enough for me.

Call me perverse, but when I looked into sailing around the world, I came across the Clipper race which sounded perfect. The Clipper route goes through the Panama Canal, following an equatorial path and travels eastwards. But then I discovered the Global Challenge – dubbed the "World's Toughest Yacht Race." The Global Challenge route goes around Cape Horn, into the Southern Ocean twice, and heads westwards, the wrong way around the world. Like a child with a new toy, I dropped the

Clipper straight away and got excited by the Global Challenge instead. I had to do it because it was tougher.

Similarly, as soon as Helen said, "Or you can ski full distance," I turned my back on the idea of skiing only the last degree. I needed to do something tougher for longer. I had learned from the Global Challenge that if you invest the time and cover a long distance over a multi-day challenge, you can't give up or get off, which makes for a richer experience - living life to the full. Endurance challenges demand 100% commitment, and even when times get tough, you have to persevere and push on through, because it's not just for a couple of days. Physically and psychologically you have to stick with it and not quit which I believe makes for a more interesting expedition, and consequently, a more interesting life. So I thought, yes, this sounds more like it.

I had to wait another year to recover from my broken Achilles, go to physio and strengthen my right leg. I also asked to complete some lung function tests to make sure my lungs and heart were clear for altitude after my pulmonary embolism. My goal, which had become a probable reality, spurred me on to get fitter and sort myself out. I was already "looking forward, not down" and allowing my future intention to drive my present decision making and fitness.

In February 2014, I flew to Norway for a Polar Training week which was pretty hard core and an uncomfortably steep learning curve. At the end of which I exclaimed: "Right, I'm not doing the South Pole, I'm not going to go to Antarctica, I hate it." I said to Alex: "Don't let me go. If I start talking nonsense about wanting to go, remind me how much I hate it." On my last night in the cabin with Helen, I said to her, "I'm not going to do it, I hate it." And she started to explain the experience which didn't sound so bad after all; in fact, it sounded pretty amazing. Thanks to Helen's stories and a stunning slide deck she subsequently showed me, I now had a vision to work towards. I had a tangible dream and an exciting future to look forward to. By the time I left, I thought fine. Fine, fine, fine, fine. I'll do it.

The "hating" it bit had been getting me down, and the incredibly powerful and emotive visualisation of skiing all the way from the Coast of Antarctica to the South Pole re-tipped the balance the other way. I had decided to step up and not give up. Tigers 1. Gremlins 0.

I now had a lot of prep to do. Before we left for Antarctica, I attended briefings and meetings about what to expect and how to manage the various elements of such an expedition. I had lessons on hygiene, nutrition, energy, cooking within a tent, clothing layers, cold injuries, hypothermia, frost bite, comms, emergency procedures, crevasse rescue, ski maintenance, navigation, kit, exercise, psychology, history, culture, waste disposal and the Antarctic Treaty. It was all important. Every taken-for-granted element of living from day to day - eating, sleeping, going to the toilet - had to be planned for in such extreme conditions. It all mattered and everything had to be just right for success to be even remotely achievable.

In planning ahead and preparing for a big expedition, I have twelve distinct aspects which I know require decent commitment from me. These roughly group under the following headings:

1. Skills training - e.g. learning to cross-country ski whilst pulling a pulk
2. Knowledge acquisition - e.g. how to manage blisters
3. Psychological preparation - e.g. talking to people who have done it to manage expectations
4. Physical fitness
5. Nutrition and weight management
6. Health maintenance and physio
7. Kit and equipment
8. Home life and admin
9. Team building or team integration
10. Communications
11. Technology - e.g. tracker, GoPro, music, etc.
12. Fun, humour and motivation - e.g. Christmas presents and vodka

Each aspect can have something like 50+ tasks associated with it, so it's quite a hefty list to accomplish in the months building up to an expedition, whilst still working and earning money in the day job. Each item needs proper care and attention; the slightest thing that has been neglected or stinted makes a lot of difference when you are in Antarctica for two months with no access to extra resources.

The **skills training** for the South Pole involved learning to cross-country ski, of course, but also pitching a tent on snow and ice, crevasse rescue techniques, cooking using MSR hybrid-fuel stoves, first-aid, cold and altitude acclimatisation and other hygiene and housekeeping factors.

The **knowledge acquisition** meant educating myself on geography, history, climate, snow and ice conditions, blister management, nutrition, ski maintenance, prevention of cold injuries, etc. A combination of the skills training and knowledge acquisition meant that at least I knew what to do and how to do it, albeit there was plenty of room for further improvement and hands-on experience.

Over the years participating in treks, travels and expeditions, I have realised how crucial the **psychological** aspect is too. I am now a converted positive psychology advocate. I believe that about 5–10% of an expedition's success is about the physical stamina and 90–95% of it relies on the mental toughness. My preparation for this was to remind myself of previous expeditions and resilience strategies but also to try to comprehend what it would be like by reading books and talking to those who had been - reminding myself not to be put off by stories of nasty experiences.

I still have a pile of wintry-looking, white dust-jacketed books by my bedside waiting to be read. I became more fascinated by the history and psychology of polar expeditions now that it was part of my life. Friends bought me books about these near-death experiences - one was anonymously posted through my letterbox about Oates' famous death in extremis, perhaps a hint from someone not wanting me to go? I read books about Scott,

Oates and Apsley Cherry-Garrard from the infamous expeditions in the 1920s, and then Shackleton, Amundsen, Fuchs and Hillary in later years, on to Fiennes, Mike Stroud and Felicity Aston more recently. It made me cold and tired just reading these books! Such fascinating stories of human endeavour, especially during the heroic age of exploration when explorers were travelling into unknown conditions and geographies with ponies and biscuits, non-technical clothing and no satellite phone or plane rescue. We have it relatively "easy" today.

I also spoke with four polar explorers from four different expeditions including a military friend who lost thumbs and toes in the attempt. He and his team had to evacuate just days from the finish. All these stories were excruciating to hear, yet still I wanted to go. They urged me onwards and forwards, despite the hardships and possible difficulties or disasters ahead.

The **physical** training for the South Pole broke down into endurance, cardio-vascular, core, balance and specific strength work on muscle groups. I trained for six days a week for the eleven months before I left. I really enjoyed this addiction to fitness and being so physically active for so long, with the specific goal driving my efforts, even in the rain and when I was knackered. I went for long runs, I went to the gym for weights work and cross-training, I trekked, cycled and swam, walked across Ireland with a backpack, did Pilates, Body Balance, Body Combat, Yoga, Body Pump, Sh'bam, Wii Fit, Sun Salutations, stretches... and a lot of tyre pulling.

Pulling tyres is perfect training for pulling a pulk uphill and into the wind as it strengthens your back muscles and core. I had two Porsche 996 Carrera 4S Pirelli 35R/18 racing tyres, which weighed 10.4 kilograms each. They were impressively large, albeit with quite a low profile. At first I trained with one tyre which we attached to my rucksack with some climbing rope (traces) around the waist belt to a large screw-eye bolt screwed into the tyre wall, fixed with a washer and nut. I felt very self-conscious initially and my first tyre pull amounted to just 0.62 miles in 12 minutes around the block. By the end of the training

I was pulling two tyres, along the beach and up and down rough terrain for 12 miles in six hours.

The tyre pulling was very sociable and I got to meet lots of people - one local bus driver grew so familiar with seeing me around he used to pull over, point me out as a local attraction and then all the passengers would turn and wave! Cars used to slow down and toot, and cause a bit of chaos. People called out from their bicycles, lorry drivers called out all sorts of things as you can imagine, and the local navy squads of cadets used to run past looking impressed and giving me a grin; it was all very encouraging and pleasing. The funnier comments were along the lines of, "Where's the rest of your car?" or "Saving up for the rest?" I met people walking their dogs who then followed the trip tracker, old ladies who scrabbled around in their purses to give me money towards my charity and one day pulling past a church, the organist rallied her contacts for an incredible £500 donation.

Pulling tyres suited my physique and capabilities. I genuinely enjoyed it as a form of fitness and I got quite emotional when I finished my last big pull. It was the end of an era, the end of hours and hours, and miles and miles of physical effort and mental solitude. I had done the beaches, forts, dunes, old military training grounds, roads, parks, footpaths in the rain, wind, sun, with music, audio books, Eddie Izzard and Radio 4. It had become an integral part of my lifestyle and defined me as a crazy local celebrity. I miss pulling my tyres and I am so tempted to put them back into action.

As I was working and often commuting to London and back - three hours each way - I had to fit in my training around that - the tyre pulling, the gym sessions, the aerobic classes - and I found that I was losing energy. I would go to a high intensity "insanity" class hardly able to walk up the stairs to the studio. I also had to bulk out to give my body insulation and fat to burn as it was predicted that we would go through 7000 calories a day, what with the cold and the physical exertion. So I ate what I liked all year and I supplemented my "eat as much as you can" diet with protein and carb shakes and bars, powders, tablets and teas. My kitchen looked like a chemistry lab; I had stuff to take before, during and after my training. Eventually I got what I call "Fat Fit," fat on the outside and fit on the inside!

For the expedition, the logistics company provided the tent, pulks, comms, first aid, harnesses, ropes, fuel and food (the food and fuel alone weighed 2.56 kilograms per day). On top of that, I spent hours and hours researching, sourcing, investigating and buying over 100 more items that I needed. I packed 54 substantial bits of kit, such as clothing and large technical equipment, plus my personal stuff (diary, pencils – pens would freeze - iPhone, headphones, GoPro, etc.), first aid, hygiene and ablution bits and pieces, including exact-specification articles such as non-water based sun-cream (other sun-creams would freeze on your skin). We were given a suggested kit list, which was a great start, but the effort and time it took to then research and buy everything was phenomenal; items were unavailable, or required a lot of investigation such as the tracking device, or were hard to find, such as the fur ruff.

A fur ruff around a hood is a very useful bit of kit. The fibres block the incoming weather creating a warm, dry micro-climate to protect the face. The effect is quite immediate and physically and psychologically comforting because all five senses receive signals of warmth and peace, instead of freezing snow and howling winds, making you feel you can cope again. Wisdom says that wolverine is the best fur because it is the most proficient and is the least likely to ice up or retain clumps of snow in its hairs, though it does stink like a wet dog when you take it off in the tent. Furriers in Alaska sell raw pelts of bear, wolf, wolverine or beaver and I had to research types of fur, the size of ruff (length to sew round a hood) the way it was finished (i.e. how much backing to leave on and whether it was prepared for a zip), how to sew it on, the prices and the import procedures. I finally sorted it and one of my favourite deliveries was a cardboard box, covered in import stickers with my wolverine fur ruff wrapped in tissue paper inside from John and Kathy Sarvis at the Alaska Fur Cache. Julian, a member of my group, was so jealous of my ruff when I posted a picture of it on Twitter that he bought a gorgeously large one to compensate, which he then had to cut while blowing it with a hair-dryer to simulate the wind!

The preparation seemed never-ending and the more I got into the details of the trip, the longer my "to do" and "to buy" lists became. One of my biggest concerns before I left was getting blisters on my feet. I had had such a miserable time in Norway that I was no doubt extra sensitive about this; my heels hadn't fully recovered - they were still pink and soft with new skin. The boot supplier was very apologetic about the original design issue and grateful for my feedback. The boots were re-designed and I was sent new boots and replacement liners free of charge. These felt right and turned out to be extremely comfortable and warm, along with the inner "mukluk" boot liners we had fitted; our socks were steaming when we took our boots off each night. But I was still worried about getting blisters so I did everything I could think of to prevent them and understand how to manage them while I was away. I bought a fantastic 370-page book called *Fixing your Feet*, written with endurance athletes very much in mind, which is about as comprehensive as it gets. I also emailed the author, John Vonhof, for personalised advice. I rubbed on tincture of benzoin from Indonesia, I tried paraffin, I walked as much as possible in bare feet to harden them up and I bought the recommended tapes and blister dressings. I even did a freezer test before I left, placing some creams and other items in my freezer overnight to see whether their composition changed. I was as prepared as I could be. I knew that my ambition to ski to the South Pole required the best preparation, the best kit and the best attitude if I was to make it. I have never been so thoroughly prepared, which in turn gave me the confidence to rock up in Antarctica feeling as ready as I could be.

On 14 November 2014 I checked in to Heathrow Airport with all my kit including my boots and skis. I was pleasantly surprised and then a little concerned at how "light" my luggage was. I'm notoriously a light packer, often turning up for events or sleepovers with just a bottle of wine and a toothbrush, and I was worried that I may have neglected something crucial, despite having lists and lists and lists. In Punta Arenas, Chile, when the logistics guys weighed our bags for the Antarctica flight, they looked surprised, then impressed and gave me the thumbs up. As it turned out, my kit was perfect. I had prepared and planned well.

Julian was very excited to be on the brink of realising his dream. A school headmaster, he had read the Ladybird book *Scott of the Antarctic* when he was six and had fallen in love with the concept of an expedition to the South Pole. That Ladybird book was a classic, as are they all, with an evocative painting on the front of Scott planting the flag at the Pole surrounded by his teammates. I can only imagine what an impression that book and the story made on a six-year-old boy! The wonder of it, the romance, the heroism, horror and then... death! It contained all the elements of a fictional adventure story but with the piquant and very real finale of disaster. Julian was moved and affected by it, and now he was on his way to reliving the story. He, himself, was going to endeavour to conquer the South Pole and his vision was about to be realised. But the anticipation and pressure had built up as a result. His greatest worry now was that his dream would be smashed - what if he didn't make it? What if, after over 30 years of thinking and dreaming about it, he didn't get there? Actually arriving at the South Pole was crucial to him. It was his definition of success (and mine). The journey would be amazing, but the getting to the finish was key.

Julian and I got on very well and we shared our hopes and fears and deepest personal thoughts about what we were about to undertake. I sensed that the worry of not making it was eating him up, spoiling the anticipation, and he was trying to relax his attitude towards it. In one of our discussions he asked me, "Paula, what is your percentage likelihood of making it to the South Pole?" I paused to think. I knew what I *felt* about it but I hadn't actually tried to quantify it. That's a headmaster for you. I explored my beliefs and hopes, skills and past experiences, and said, "Ninety-nine per cent." Julian was quite shocked it was so high, but also pleasantly surprised by my answer. *"Really*?! That's quite high..." he tailed off in hope. I explained that I felt that was a reasonable figure, and barring a curve ball, I felt that I had trained enough, that I understood what the challenges were which lay ahead, that I knew I was made of strong stuff and 99% was my realistic but *feasible belief*.

Julian brightened up. He had been trying to diminish his hope and dampen his excitement in case he failed. **But you don't set out to fail. You set out to finish**. Getting to the actual South Pole was a very important part of the "ski to the South Pole" expedition. Anything less than that would have been a grand experience, but not actually the point. I had prepared, planned and trained for the whole thing with 100% commitment, looking forward, not down. In fact I believe that you need to prepare for going *beyond* the finish line, otherwise your energy, physical effort and mental fortitude might just give out at the last hurdle. In reality we had to ski for six days longer than I had anticipated, so aiming beyond the finish, looking forward not down, was key to my mind-set at the end.

Julian, looking much happier and more liberated, approved of my explanation, acknowledged that my belief was indeed feasible and recalibrated his own likelihood of success. We were now both about to set off on the toughest challenge of our lives, with 99% hope beating in our hearts... would we be proven right or wrong?

On 22 November, with much excitement and trepidation in our hearts, we were told we were flying from Chile to Union Glacier. The day had come when we would set foot on Antarctica. No more emails and phone calls home. No more "civilisation." We were heading off to the coldest continent in the world.

We flew out on a beautiful beast that I fell in love with - the Ilyushin IL76 commercial freighter plane, a mammoth, rudimentary, Russian work-horse with drooping wings and a glass-panelled nose. I was so excited. Just flying on that plane was an experience in itself. There were two portholes in the main fuselage and with a GoPro attached to the nose of the plane with a live camera feed to the main screen, we were able to watch the view as it changed from Chile, to the Southern Ocean, to ice-floes, to solid ice. We edged nearer and nearer to this most amazing of places and the atmosphere on the plane was intense. Fifteen minutes before landing, the flight crew switched off the heating so we could put on our polar gear in readiness. Nerves took over from the excitement; now the plane was buzzing with panic as we tried to put on our cumbersome jackets, boots, hats, gloves and goggles for the first time in anger.

At Union Glacier we spent a couple of days doing more prep and went on a shake-down ski trip with an overnight camp. More crevasse rescue practice and more final, final details. I felt so ready that I was bursting with anticipation, bordering on frustration. It had been a year in the making, two years since I had first spoken with Helen, and finally, the moment had come.

On 25 November, we took a Twin Otter ski-plane out of Union Glacier and landed at the coast of Antarctica at 82 degrees, 20 minutes south. The Twin Otter took off and waggled goodbye and we were finally alone, surrounded by snow and ice. It was a truly awesome sight and remained so for the next 46 days. Blue sky and white ice, 24 hours a day, as far as the eye could see. Suddenly, there was a huge "Whoomph" like a distant explosion. We all swore, expecting to get swallowed by a crevasse opening up under our feet. It was a horizontal snow layer collapse! Antarctica was welcoming us.

We skied for nearly nine hours a day, in seven 75-minute blocks, with a ten-minute break in between each leg, typically starting at 0900 and stopping at about 1930 each day after 12 hours out in the elements. Housekeeping took five hours; making camp, cooking, and so on, totalling to 17 hours a day, leaving just seven hours for personal time and sleeping. It wasn't much. My main impression was how relentless it was.

We skied uphill and into the wind for the majority of the expedition, ascending 3,300 metres with the wind blowing down off the polar plateau, creating a buffeting resistance on the way to the pole. The snow conditions also made a difference to the skiing experience each hour. Sometimes the surface made the hauling easy and sometimes it made it twice as hard and drained all our energy. Then there was the sastrugi to contend with. Sastrugi are snow formations shaped by the wind into hard waves or ridges, sometimes a few centimetres deep, sometimes a few metres. Sometimes they look like a school of frozen, leaping dolphins. It proved easier to ski perpendicular over the ridge tops than up and down the fissures in parallel with them, as this would occasionally cause a loss of control as we slid into the dips. I fell over most frequently when there was a white out, flat light, and I couldn't tell where the sastrugi were and therefore where my skis were going.

Inevitably, falling over happened most often on the worst days with the poorest visibility and lack of definition and no motivational sunshine. Day Nine was our worst day overall for average pace:

> *Wednesday 3 December. Day Nine. 18 knots wind. 19.1 km. 8 hours 50 minutes. Average pace 2.16 km.*
>
> *Toughest day yet. White out, flat light and snowed most of the day – which doesn't help at all. Two problems there –*
> *Rob (the guide) can't see a good line to take us on so we have many more lumps and bumps to manoeuvre over*
> *We can't see the ground dead in front of us so often get caught by surprise by a dip, groove, bump or hill*
> *I started the day in good spirits – enjoying the snow... But then I kept falling over, which got to me – tiring, frustrating, painful, slows me down – grrrr! Must have fallen 30x in total, sometimes 5/6 times in one 75-minute stint.*
> *So then, what with the poor vis, the strain on my shoulders and falling a lot, I began to not enjoy the day so much! Was a little bit left behind on the last 3 legs because of falling, but could keep up otherwise.*

There are the obvious challenges with falling over, like the pain and bruising, and the slowness and frustration, but the less obvious challenge is not to get too tired or sweaty trying to get back up. When it is the sixth time in an hour, your skis are stuck in a curved hollow, you are 48 years old and harnessed to an 80 kilogram pulk, it is not easy to get up and stay up. I would often build up some heat doing this, and sweat on the body then freezes on your skin, which is not good. Also goggles steam up and then freeze over which you haven't got time to do anything about. (We had a perfectly sensible team rule which was to only stop at the official break times; otherwise we would have faffed too much along the way which would slow down our overall progress).

On the worst days, in flat light, my goggles would freeze over so I was skiing blindly, peering through a tiny 1 cm x 1 cm clear patch by my nose; my skis would unexpectedly slide down a fissure and I would fall suddenly backwards, winded and crashing down on my hip or coccyx. I partly put this down to low ski confidence and the more timid I got, of course, the more I fell backwards. It was a vicious circle that I needed to re-wind. One thing I did to try and counteract this was to look forwards - to where I wanted to be - rather than down, something I had learned while snow-boarding. If I aimed for the clear snow ahead of me, rather than worrying about the one metre of snow that I was trying to tackle or turn in, then my body posture and confidence improved. If I looked forwards, towards my goal, my mind and body lined up better and I was less likely to fall. You get what you focus on. It certainly helped me to be more punchy and confident and less likely to hesitate and fall backwards.

Look forward, not down is about actually looking ahead as well as looking towards something positive, to the break, or the sun coming out and not being downcast each time you fall. It is about aiming towards where you want to be - physically and mentally. Another mantra was born to add to my mental collection.

It wasn't until Day 15 I felt that I had finally cracked it and was in control.

Paula Reid

Chapter 10
Pain is Temporary, Pride is Forever

The extreme cold in Antarctica - ranging from -20° down to -40° Centigrade plus wind-chill - was our biggest enemy. Exposure to the cold, or cold injuries, potentially meant a medical evacuation and a failure to finish, as well as the possibility of a life-long injury such as lost fingers or toes.

Infamous images and stories abound of black noses, swollen thumbs and sawn-off digits immortalised in books and films about Scott of the Antarctic, Oates ("I'm going outside, I may be some time"), Ranulph Fiennes, Joe Simpson (*Touching the Void*) and the recent *Everest* film graphically depicting the 1996 disaster when eight people got caught in a blizzard and died of exposure on the mountain. Understanding and appreciating the scientific and medical facts around cold injuries, as well as the emotional and haunting stories of human endeavour, meant that committing to undertake the "South Pole Full Distance" took a lot of resolve and strength of mind with eyes wide open to the potential risks. The whole trip carried a "DANGER. PROCEED WITH EXTREME CAUTION" hazard sign. There were multitudinous things that could go wrong and many were due to the extremes of the cold environment. One thing that the guides, experts and medics were all concerned about in particular was "Polar Thigh."

"Polar Thigh" is a relatively new term classified as a "non-freezing cold injury" (NFCI), unlike frost bite, brought about by the extreme cold and on the rare occasions that it does occur, it seems to only happen on a polar expedition - in other words in the Arctic or Antarctic, not for instance on Everest or any of the other long, winter, extreme climbs or treks. There is currently no definite single opinion about what exactly causes it, but possible explanations include the repetitive forward-back scissoring movement of skiing, as opposed to trekking or climbing, which is likely to affect the large thigh muscles. There is also the long exposure to the cold; skiing full distance to the South Pole typically involves skiing into the wind for often 12 hours a day, for 40–60 days at a time. Some fault the close layered clothing system, modern tech thermals and base layers, perhaps trapping sweat which then cools off, especially on exposed thighs which aren't encased in boots or the upper-body layers and jacket. Or the fact that these materials stretch thinner as your thigh pushes forward against the clothing on each stride, providing less protection. There is even mention of the fine hairs on thighs which may cause friction within the tight confines of a restrictive base layer. Fascinating stuff.

Polar Thigh can result in medical evacuation and the end of the trip, especially if it gets infected. So naturally, the medics, guides and expedition personnel were concerned about this phenomenon and we had official and unofficial conversations around it. We were advised to wear "down skirts" over our usual daytime clothing (thermal base layers and windproof salopettes) and we were shown photos to inform us as to what to look out for. It was a concern to all of us as it could mean not getting to the South Pole which is rather key in a "ski to the South Pole" objective.

Unluckily I got Polar Thigh on Day 7.

We had had quite an unexpectedly tough start to the expedition. There were more sastrugi than we were expecting which made the going physically and technically demanding, and we experienced a fair bit of falling snow (unusual as Antarctica is classified as a desert) and wind. At the end of each day, once we were in our tents and having done the urgent jobs, we would sit with a hot muscle-recovery drink while the next pan of water was boiling, and do some hygiene/housekeeping - perhaps cleaning with a wet wipe or flannel, checking our bodies for wear and tear, and fixing feet with plasters, tape or Compeeds. In changing my base layer, I noticed red lumps all over and all around my thighs. Like 50 chilblains on each thigh. At this stage they were slightly raised, hot and itchy which was bad enough in fluctuating temperatures and wearing some synthetic fibres. It drove me nuts, but at this point, I didn't think it was Polar Thigh. I just thought my legs were reacting from the cold and heat, sensitive to the changing temperatures, hard work and tough days. I took some antihistamine which helped ease the discomfort.

Over the next few days the individual "chilblains" joined together to form big red welts, as much as 10cm across; still just hot and itchy, though no pain. However, the medics were beginning to talk about medical evacuation and Polar Thigh on the satellite phone to me and this got me more concerned than I actually was. I didn't think it was Polar Thigh because it looked so innocuous initially and I felt fine. But mentally, the talk of medevacking was quite upsetting. What was some discomfort on my legs was now taking on a more serious and dark significance. Thoughts around quitting and being flown out were unwelcomingly invading my mind, like dark, spreading tendrils inside my head, gripping my positive thoughts in a tight, negative embrace. One evening I talked to the medics via the satellite phone for an hour, and instead of cheering me up with their well-intentioned sympathy, all the "fuss" and sympathy made me feel weaker and more vulnerable with less chance of success. Their concern was catching and disempowering.

The next day skiing was a tough day with white light, poor visibility and lots of falling over, sweating and swearing to get up each time. I couldn't help thinking, "Why am I bothering if I'm going to be medevacked any day now?" It's difficult enough mentally and physically to get through a challenging day, but when you have invasive and siren-like thoughts luring you towards an exit, it is very hard to resist. I could feel myself getting physically weaker each time I just thought about quitting. I mentally struggled all day. This was no good at all. The give-up gremlins were beginning to take a hold.

That night I was in a dark mood. I was physically tired and cold, and mentally battling with the idea of a medevac. I was not ready to quit. I was not even ready to *think* about quitting. It was destabilising my positive energy and the positive psychology that I needed to continue in such harsh and relentless circumstances. I had a chat with our team leader, who also had excellent medical experience in dealing with trauma in the field of battle. He had certainly seen and dealt with much worse than this, and I wasn't a giving up type of girl. I explained that I would quit if I had to, as a responsible and reasonable thing to do if there was a definite call to do so, if I was in serious jeopardy or letting the team down with my inability to cope, but right now, quitting was not an option and not a decision I would take lightly. He nodded in understanding. He got it. He knew then I had a high pain threshold and a high endurance threshold. That I was mentally strong. That I believed in stepping up not giving up when it came to the crunch. I think from then on I was treated as a survivor rather than a victim, and our whole approach to my Polar Thigh changed.

He explained that I mainly needed to manage the pain and the potential for infection if I had a hope of continuing. Looking at it purely from this point of view suddenly cleared thoughts of a medevac. All I had to do was manage the pain and manage the hygiene and I would probably be OK. This made sense and was doable. This was something I could focus on and act upon to the best of my ability. This didn't muck around with my head.

I realised when I got home afterwards that we spend so much effort with the physical aspects of an injury - the look of the trauma, whether it looks better or worse than before, what to put on it, what pills to take, what dressings and lotions are best - that we neglect the mental aspect. We manage the pain *but we don't manage the brain.*

95% of this is about attitude. That's why I believe in **Choose your Attitude**. That's why I believe that **Pain is temporary, Pride is Forever** and that's why I now also believe that we should "**manage the pain AND manage the brain.**" When I broke my Achilles tendon and got a pulmonary embolism, all the attention was on the physical. I had X-Rays, MRIs, heart and lung function tests, morphine, warfarin injections, crutches and a boot. But nothing for what was going on inside my head.

So when I was diagnosed with Polar Thigh in Antarctica, it wasn't until I sorted my head out that I began to feel better. I knew that if I could manage the pain, manage the cleanliness to avoid infection AND choose my attitude (or manage my brain), then I could continue and not quit. So I did.

Day 31 was Christmas Day and we were hoping to reach our second resupply drop of food and fuel including Christmas food, decorations and presents as well as sloe gin, whiskey, Croatian Liquor and toffee vodka! We were behind schedule and had a hard push of over 25 kilometres to get there in time. This was our longest day skiing in the 46 days and unfortunately there was a biggish uphill slog at the end. I was leading at this point and it was sheer determination to get to the Christmas food and vodka before the end of Christmas Day that drove me up that hill. A bamboo flag marked the spot and didn't seem to get any nearer for hours, but inch by inch we got closer and reached our Christmas resupply at 2230 with 1½ hours left to celebrate!

It was a very surreal but fantastic Christmas as we sat in our red tents parked in the middle of a huge white snowfield with the sentimental sound of Christmas carols drifting out into the frozen air from our iPhones. I wondered what it would have looked and sounded like from space or if aliens had been watching. We were in our own isolated and yet intimate world and it was the most incredible, unique experience. That and Christmas Day in the Southern Ocean! We ate rehydrated chicken, mash and peas (as close to a Christmas dinner as we could muster), gave each other presents and hugs, hung up our decorations, drank and sang. It was very merry and cosy.

Knowing that the next day we wouldn't be moving - we had to wait for a plane to come and pick up one of our party - we also looked forward to a lie-in the next morning. It was nice to have some time off and enjoy Boxing Day, but we were frustrated and keen to move on. My legs were also getting worse and worse every day we were out there and exposed to the cold. On Boxing Day I developed large, bubble blisters on my thighs which had to be pierced and drained so I could ski again. This was a mildly painful business - helped with a few drams of whisky - but was also the start of definite pain in my thighs and since the skin had now been broken, the chance of infection increased.

Two-and-a-half days later the weather finally cleared enough for a plane to take off from Union Glacier and land at our resupply location. I could have got on the flight with my teammate and it was certainly a very tempting and emotional prospect, but I chose to Look Forward and ski on. We had about 11–12 days to go with luck. It was going to be tough. On Day 34 at 1530 local time, we pushed on, one man down.

The toughest day was Day 35. On a normal day the challenge was hard enough: skiing uphill, into the wind, in -40°C with wind chill, pulling an 80 kilogram pulk for 12 hours. My back would start to ache on the first leg of each day - within 75 minutes of setting off - so then I would start popping the painkillers. As the days wore on, we got technically better at skiing, but more weary, thin and desperate to finish. We were losing weight (I lost 15 kilograms during the 46-day trip) and it gets colder as you approach the South Pole.

On Day 35, we weren't close enough to the South Pole to start feeling good about it and we'd been doggedly trudging on for what felt like forever. We had left in November and it was now nearly January. Initially we had hoped to finish in 40 days, so knowing that it was Day 35 and we still had 11 days to go was psychologically difficult. Day 35 was one of those especially mean days. Latitude 87° to 88° South is notoriously difficult because of the geographical features and weather which affect the snow conditions. We rarely had "sticky snow" but here we did and it cleaves to the loaded pulks making them even harder to drag. Deep sastrugi featured a lot here too. We had to pull our pulks up and over or around the larger formations. Sometimes the pulks tip over on the camber or edges of the sastrugi, which means stopping and heaving at the pulk to upright it again. This in turn makes you hot and sweaty which then condenses and freezes on your body, creating ice sheets on your jacket lining and freezing inside your goggles so you can't see. Meanwhile my back and legs were very, very painful and the condition of my thighs was deteriorating each day with the risk of infection weighing on my mind. Would I even make it to the Pole after all this effort?

29 December. Day 35. 8 hrs, 50 mins skiing. 23 km.
Tough ol' day. They do say that it gets tough at latitude 87 degrees South and it did. Tough yesterday afternoon for the three legs we did and tough all day today. A lot of uphill and sticky snow causing friction and a lot of sastrugi.
Back was killing me – especially between the shoulders. Owwww!
Legs hurt a bit too – Rob had pierced, drained and dressed about 10 blisters on my thighs the day before and all a bit sore.
Managed 23 km today tho'.

30 December. Day 36. Julian's birthday. 8 hrs, 50 mins skiing. 23.5 km. Average pace 2.66 km per hour.
Another tough day!! Tho' weather was still OK thank goodness. Blue sky all day and clear viz.
But snow still sticky, and lots of sastrugi and my back still really hurting, so I was on paracetamol, Nurofen and Codeine today! Whatever it takes!

I lead two of the legs, lost the will to live on leg 5 (worst leg?) and then leg 7 was uphill and monster sastrugi. Aaahh!

Thighs still sore too.

Nose sore.

But hey, did 23.5 km and calculate only 10 days to go...

Notice the positive end to each diary entry? Choose your attitude.

We were constantly calculating times, distances, days done and days to go; it was central to our lives during the whole expedition, and to our happiness. We used to have big debates in the evening about the maths, trying to make it work in our favour and generally doing some creative accounting to give us hope of a quicker finish.

The flesh in my thighs got ulcerated and I had large, open wounds on the tops and insides of both thighs. The pain was getting unbearable, attacking my tissue, muscles and nervous system.

Day by day, hour by hour, we skied on. It was very satisfying to eat up the kilometres in the last few days. Completing degrees of latitude were large motivational markers and on the 5th of January, Day 42, we crossed from 88° to 89° South and were finally on our last degree. I was up and at 'em that morning, outside and busting to get started at 0830.

Until those last few days I had been distracting myself by listening to music (pumped and mellow), Eddie Izzard, the complete works of Sir Arthur Conan Doyle and Bill Bryson's *A Short History of Nearly Everything*, but now I turned it all off and put the headphones away: re-engaging my senses with what I was doing and what I was achieving, soaking up the awesomeness of my last few days skiing in Antarctica; seizing the day and savouring the moment; recognising that I was well and truly living life to the full in every sense. This was about the big stuff, the stuff that dreams are made of - the wonder of Antarctica, the fantastic environment, the romantic and inspirational history, the fact we were nearly there, the sadness of a journey's end, the almost unbearable pain, and me and my struggle. It got fairly emotional and almost overwhelming. If I thought too profoundly about what I was doing, I had to choke back my sobbing, my face aching from the battle not to cry. The achievement was so close, but the pain was increasing. **Pain is Temporary, Pride is Forever** was not yet realised, but the thought of achieving it kept me going. I was not going to give up now.

For the last four or five days, my legs were extremely, unbearably painful. I really don't think I could have gone on another day and knowing that the end was near helped me push on. It was most painful setting up the tent, being in the tent and breaking camp because every time I had to bend or kneel, my thighs stretched. By the time we set off each morning, I was crying my eyes out, which then froze my goggles. Once we were underway, and I skied carefully, as long as I just concentrated on putting one ski in front of the other and took plenty of painkillers each time we stopped, I could just about cope. Even when we drew near to the Pole, I couldn't look at it or think about it because I knew that would be the end of my courage. I had to just keep pushing. I got slower, but still skied on. I dug deeper than I knew I could. Polar Thigh made the whole challenge three times harder, as if skiing to the South Pole for 46 days wasn't hard enough. I was in survival mode; one step at a time. I persevered. If I allowed myself to think that we were nearly there, I knew I would have lost the shreds of resolve I had left.

At 24 kilometres out, on a clear day, you can see the South Pole - specifically, small black dots of the Antarctic Research Station on the horizon. We saw it the day before we got there...

> *8 January 2015. Day 45. 25.9 km.*
> *14.5 km from finish!*
> *Could see station on leg 5 but then it got cloudy and it all disappeared.*

I was hurting a lot towards the end of the day and suggested others went ahead.

I don't think I could have done another day or two. The timing's been incredible. It's been awful, over-shadowing the experience from Day 7.

[It's the] last night. Last yukky dinner (mash and cheese), last very difficult sleep in a sleeping bag covered in hydrocortisone cream, aloe vera gel, Granuflex, plasters, gunk. Turning over hurts. Sleeping with my thighs together hurts. Kneeling especially hurts, i.e. having a pee. Have decided that at S.P, I shall just stay awake all night in the main tent to save all the pain. Getting up and out in the morning each day is the worst...

So we slept, for the last time, just a few kilometres away from the South Pole and the end of our amazing expedition. But it was a rough night:

FRIDAY 9 JANUARY 2015. Day 46! LAST DAY!! 14.5 km
Up at 0600 and straight on the codeine. 2 before breakfast. Thighs streaming with coffee coloured gunk. Any overnight healing getting torn apart each time I move.

It had been a bad night and I must have been a bit delirious.

I talked in my sleep.

'Newall' kept telling me to turn over [Newall, skiing solo, had finished about four days before]. I think I must have obeyed him because I know I had been tossing and turning in my sleeping bag.

My mouth was v.v. dry and kept having to drink thermos water.

Peed 3x. Disaster!

But. The. Last. Day.

14.5 km to go.

Four legs of 75 minutes each.

My tent mate and I set about the two-hour morning routine – for the last time! Yay! We were uber-efficient by now, having done this twice a day for 45 days. First job was to put the kettle on for a nice cup of tea. Always a winner. We lit our MSR liquid-fuel stove and got the very satisfying roar of the gas flame. Before the tent walls started dripping down our necks, we scraped off as much ice as we could, banging the top to shake off the snow. Big slabs slid off with a hiss and it got lighter inside. Wondering what the weather was going to be like for our last push, I shouted out to ask the boys... Perfect! Blue sky and sun, no wind. Temp. -40 degrees Centigrade.

I enjoyed my last cup of tea while we boiled water for an hour – we needed less today anticipating only a 2/3 day. I wasn't getting on with the Porridge so I skipped it – it was the last day after all – and ate some nutritional bars instead. My daily snack bag of peanuts, chocolate, energy blocks and cheese was ready to sustain me until we got there. I looked in the mirror. Crusty nose and sun-blasted cheeks and 14 kilos lighter, not a pretty sight, but OK considering. I didn't bother checking my thighs, I knew they were bad and I only had to survive one more day.

Once the housekeeping was done, we checked in with the other tent to see when they would be ready to break camp. The boys were all set, it was time to venture out of our warm, snuggly nest and into the freezing cold. We were all keen to crack on today.

Packing up hurt a lot with all the bending over and bending down and I was soon crying with the pain, making my goggles condense and freeze. I would now have very limited vision until I had a chance to change the lens and there was no point doing that until I had control of my tears.

I just had to pull through, grit my teeth, gather my resilience, be determined, and get on with it:

Set off in great deal of pain.
Frozen goggles.
Hands freezing.

Desp. for pee.
All uphill.
So. Survival time.
Survival only. More codeine. One step at a time, focused on just 4" snow ahead, ploughing away, ignoring the sight of the SP buildings – just dark dots on the horizon - so I could concentrate on putting one foot in front of the other and not give up.

The first leg was all uphill. My hands were freezing, my body was unusually cold, I had frozen goggles and annoyingly I was desperate for another wee. Despite our best, multiple efforts to use an especially adapted type of she-wee called a Whizz Freedom, extended with some rubber tubing by the mechanics back at Union Glacier, we girls had to resort to peeing the old fashioned way...

1st stop, pee.
Skis off (hurts to bend down).
Harness off (difficult to unclip with freezing and numb fingers).
Bergans jacket off – trying to rest it on top of pulk so doesn't blow away or get snowy. Wind starts to freeze your back. [At this point I was just in a thin thermal top].
Down skirt off (hard to step out of because of thighs)
Salopettes down – v. cold and exposed now.
Down jacket on.
...Now, can go for a pee! Reverse all that then '2 minutes' call to go off again!

On the first ten-minute stop I only had time to have a pee and put on an extra layer - no time to clear my goggles, eat or drink, so I set off for my second 75-minute leg still with frozen vision, following the orange bit of gaffer tape attached to the pulk in front. It was very hard to keep going but at least I had fixed three things: put on my down-filled Gilet; taken more painkillers which were masking much of my pain and relieved myself! Small, but significant, mercies. It was all uphill again so I slowly plodded on. Time was excruciatingly slow; so near, and yet so far. No relaxing yet…

On the second stop I had time to change the lens of my goggles - hurray! and I could see again. I also drank some hot protein drink and inelegantly shoved several Probar "bolt block" energy cubes into my mouth. I had been getting a high off them for the last six weeks and was worried in case I was forming an addiction for these and Codeine. Rob, our guide, reckoned that the next leg would be a short one - just 2.5 kilometres instead of 3.5 - as there was a Waypoint ahead where we had to phone in to the South Pole reception party. It was getting very real and exciting. Time went slowly. There was still a long way to go. I was deteriorating but persevering.

Eventually I saw a yellowish thing ahead, which gradually got closer and clearer. The other three were waiting for me by it. I had a fresh goggle lens in and could see. I looked, and saw the South Pole station on my right for the first time, and a big, yellow sign ahead – "Welcome to the South Pole!" What a ridiculous and welcome sight, but still five kilometres to go.

We then had to follow a pisted track which we were not allowed to veer off because we were in an area of scientific research. From this point on we were not allowed to leave anything in the snow, not even pee. There were flags and boundary signs to our left, and ahead and to our right were a mix of structures at first indistinct, but each time I allowed myself to look up, became more defined. These were the first man-made constructions we had seen apart from our tents and the planes for 46 days. Up ahead there was the Antarctic Research Station (two low, grey buildings), three radio telescopes and observatories, a collection of blue and red tents, a load of cargo, crates, containers, vehicles and two smaller grey huts. We were not yet actually at the South Pole.

As a team of four, we all agreed to ski in together. At this point I was by far the slowest and the others generously slowed down and kept abreast of me. My throat was feeling itchy and tickly; I think it was because I was trying not to cry. I'll never forget that moment. Skiing slowly and so painfully towards the South Pole, looking left and right to keep in line with my fellow team members, getting nearer and nearer to the semi-circle of flags of Antarctic Treaty Nations and the ceremonial South Pole.

We walked through the semi-circle of flags. We got to the South Pole mirror ball, paused, looked at each other, counted to three then all touched it at the same time. We had arrived.

I had difficulty in quite taking in where I was and how I'd got there, and then moments of almost breaking down and sobbing and trying to battle with myself not to cry.

We hugged a lot, immensely relieved and proud, and then headed off for a last pull, towards the cold beer and champagne waiting for us.

It was so, so painful. But I made it. And the pride of skiing full distance to the South Pole will stay with me forever.

* * *

Six months after I first contracted Polar Thigh, my wounds finally healed over.

I get asked lots of questions about my experience and especially "Paula Thigh" as it's now known. People are fascinated by it physically and fascinated by the resilience it provoked in me. Occasionally, I get asked whether it was worth it. Was it worth continuing with such pain and perhaps further damaging my legs in the enduring cold? How did I not quit?

For me - and this is very much a personal point of view - it was very much worth it. I have some pretty serious scars on my thighs, but in fact, I am proud of how I got them and how unique they are. I see them as battle scars or badges of honour. Many people have scars for all sorts of different reasons; that's OK. We are human and diverse and interesting.

I would not have jeopardised my life. Trying to discuss "body part value" versus the definition of success is a strange concept, yet we honestly had conversations in Antarctica around, "What would you be prepared to have happen to you before you quit?" Frostbite was likely, so we discussed, as responsible individuals, "Would you be prepared to lose a toe, a finger, the tip of your nose to frostbite?" and for me, the answer is no. There were physical injuries that I would have bailed out for. I managed my thighs and for me, I made the right decisions. Pain is temporary, pride is forever. I will never, ever, lose the moment of being at the South Pole, on the 9th of January 2015, with tears in my eyes, standing (ridiculously) in my Union Jack dress and feeling as proud as punch.

It had been an enriching journey to the South Pole, and also in preparing beforehand and recovering afterwards. The expedition was extremely stretchy and demanding, relentlessly harrowing, painful and traumatic; wonderful, extraordinary and emotional, and I wouldn't have missed it for the world because it was about living life to the full - the pain and the gain.

Paula Reid

Chapter 11
Full Circle

"Is it normal to feel very flat, slightly depressed and have the feeling that everything is so insignificant here?" asked my friend Kelly on her return after cycling from Vietnam to Cambodia to raise money for Macmillan nurses. My answer was, "Yes, totally normal." In fact, she puts it very well. This is the down side of the activity, adventure, thrills and adrenaline rushes. Feeling very flat, slightly depressed, and a sense of the insignificance of ordinary life when it's all over.

On coming back from the Global Challenge round-the-world yacht race, we went from being courageous and adventurous round-the-world yachtsmen and women, with all the exaltation and glory that comes with that, to being ordinary, out of work, ex-sailors. We had been living on the edge for ten months, risking our lives, sailing the high seas, watched by tens of thousands of people, sailing among pods of dolphins and whales, visiting Sydney, Cape Town, Argentina and New Zealand, without any bills to pay, emails to answer or piles of ironing to do. We had lived in our own microcosm of high adventure, cut off from reality. We hadn't had to think, or work, or decide what to wear or what to eat for nearly a year. It was almost like being children again without a care apart from sailing and winning. We had fun, banter and amazing wild parties; we had slept under the stars, seen the Southern Lights and Milky Way, rounded Cape Horn, and watched the luminescence trailing off dolphins in the moonlight every night. We had successfully carried out two medevacs and survived many accidents, a knock-over, pirates and tornados. It was a crazy, topsy-turvy, extreme lifestyle. We were a close-knit family who knew each other inside out. We felt like rock-stars. In Portsmouth we were treated like returning heroes. There were celebrations, awards, fans, family, and media interviews. We cried, we hugged, we drank, and we celebrated. And then... it stopped. We all went home.

We went home to normality - in fact something harder than normality, which involved bills and finding work, as well as coming to terms with life after the Global Challenge.

The main difficulty was the contrast between the adrenaline-filled, life or death, living on the edge sharpness and the blurry comfort of everyday, safe, homely routine. This was hard also for the families and loved ones, the mothers and children and husbands, who had supported us and coped without us for ten months, and who were desperate to have us home again. And we were also desperate to see them, we loved them. It was just very hard to make that transition, and as my friend Kelly quite rightly puts it, you do feel flat and slightly depressed. It's the post-event blues.

The adaptation required is probably comparable to coming out of the army or prison. We suddenly had to carry the burden of being independent, responsible and decisive and grapple with the subtle complexities of life again. We had to switch on our emails and deal with the spam in our inboxes. We had to build our finances back up because we had blown so much on realising our dream. We had to get a normal job which didn't involve working on the foredeck of a racing yacht in a competitive round-the-world yacht race. We had to open all our post which was 95% junk or bills, relearn to cook properly, eat properly, dress smartly and speak nicely. Our skipper called it "reintegration to polite society." Here is an excerpt from his speech warning us about the changes ahead:

> *We will all need to continue to remember our Ps and Qs and re-establish a respect for our elders and females present. However my main concern regards table manners... cutlery should be held correctly and not used to emphasise one's point... Trouser trumping or for that matter any voluntary or involuntary orifice utterance will be heavily frowned upon, as will any pride associated with such activity. Furthermore the hanging of one's laundry from furniture will provoke disapproval from others...Showering, shaving and the wearing of clean clothes will soon be expected of us all. No longer will it be a matter of competition as to the length of time one has avoided the shower, changed one's underwear or even slept in one's foulies...*

Thanks to Clive Cosby, Skipper, Team Stelmar

Another part of the problem is that you have fulfilled your dream; it is time to wake up and the dream is no longer there to look forward to. Maybe you had had a dream of sailing around the world since you watched boats sail past your bedroom window when you were a child; maybe you had been inspired by the Ladybird book *Scott of the Antarctic*; maybe Mont Blanc had been calling you since you went to Chamonix when you were ten; maybe you were inspired by your grandfather... The dream had been there, burning brightly, giving you hope and ambition that one day would be fulfilled.

The decision to go for your dream is huge. The years of thinking and wishing are over. It's time to take action. So you talk to your family and friends and somehow get their approval or agreement. You make the big commitment and sign up. The dream now becomes a reality; it feels totally different now. It is actually going to happen after all the imagining and talking. Everyone you meet is now asking you about it... you feel like a minor celebrity, basking in the glow of admiration, and you haven't even done anything yet! At dinner parties and down the pub your friends are asking all about the challenge, what it involves, how the training is going, who the other people are and how you are feeling. It's just something for them to talk about, but for you, it is real, you are the centre of the attention and the pressure accumulates to actually do the thing. The expectation builds up around you. You had better have an amazing time...

Then you do the thing - the adventure, the expedition, the challenge, the life changing, courageous thing - and it is a vibrantly rich experience which makes you feel fully alive, you are pushed to limits beyond imagining, you make lifelong friendships, you laugh and cry together and save each other's lives, you push and grow, feel deeply, dig deeply, strain, stretch, suffer and celebrate. It's an extraordinary time. You have never seen so much, felt so deeply before. You are on a high.

Then you finish and come home. At first it's all good: there is a welcome home, a celebration, perhaps a party. Most people want to hear all about it, you wax lyrical, excited to share, you show them your amazing photos and scars, drink champagne with South Pole ice-cubes, tell them about the time when... but they weren't actually there and there is only so much story-telling you can do. You long for your old adventure buddies who were there and who totally get all your anecdotes and in-trip jokes and vulnerable moments. You have complex and controversial thoughts about courage, and death, quitting, and the edge, but you can't really share these comfortably with people when you get back. You feel very different, much older in experience than before you left; you have seen and done bigger and deeper stuff than most people you left behind.

Then life moves on. You can't keep banging on about it. The husbands and wives and friends and children will roll their eyes when you once more go on about when you skied to the South Pole. Yeah, yeah, yeah. The neighbours have heard it all before, and you can't keep finding new hairdressers and taxi drivers to tell...

So there are all sorts of issues with the coming back thing. Coming back to face reality. Coming back after the guts and the glory have held you together and kept you motivated for a year. Coming back to face the music at home. Coming back from a racing high to post-race blues.

It's hard enough coming back if you have succeeded, but coming back after a failure can be even tougher. In the very first round-the-world yacht race - the Sunday Times Golden Globe in 1968 - nine courageous men set off to sail solo, non-stop, all the way around the world, a feat that had never been attempted before, and only one man finished. As brilliantly described in the aptly entitled *A Voyage for Madmen* by Peter Nichols and also sensitively portrayed in the TV documentary *Deep Water*, British competitor Donald Crowhurst started off well and in the hope of winning the not inconsiderable prize money to save his flailing business, but soon encountered difficulty and eventually secretly stopped racing whilst pretending to continue by falsifying his reported positions. The mental and physical conflict eventually drove him to insanity and he committed suicide. There is fame and fortune and glory on the one hand, and disappointment and disaster on the other; intense and dramatic contrast between the hope and expectation riding high, and then failure, losing the competition and coming home a fallen hero. For Crowhurst, the option of returning home to his wife and children, having spent all their hopes on a boat, broke and a failure, was untenable.

The other competitor who famously struggled with the mental challenge at the end, for a different reason, was Bernard Moitessier. Also with a wife and children waiting for his return home in France, Bernard was winning the race and likely to finish first and bag the prize money, but couldn't face actually finishing. He had a different mental battle storming in his head from Donald Crowhurst and instead of pulling up and quitting, he decided to *continue past* the finish line and sail on to Tahiti instead. His message:

"Parce que je suis heureux en mer et peut-etre pour sauver mon ame"

(Because I am happy at sea and perhaps to save my soul)

One could say that these reactions are selfish and do not take into account the sacrifices and hopes of their families, but I think that these men were suffering mentally. They could not cope with the reality of finishing, and the pressures and expectations of themselves and the people they loved. It is hard enough to return a winner, or a finisher, but to return as someone who has tried with all their heart and soul and then "failed" ... that is the hardest of all. Knowing that you have to live with yourself, and with the questions and concerns of everyone there to meet you - it takes a very strong person to deal with it. For Moitessier, he just couldn't face finishing.

When I finished the Global Challenge, I was disappointed but not altogether disheartened to be on the boat that finished sixth out of the twelve competitors. We had reasons why we were sixth and I could live with them. I knew that we had performed brilliantly. I knew that I had given it my best and I was proud because that was the maximum I could have asked of myself. I believe that my whole team were happy and content with our performance, the way we sailed and the way we had behaved for the last ten months. We had integrity and humility, we had been respectful and hardworking, and we had delivered on leadership and teamwork. Our sixth place result was acceptable; indeed, our revised goal after our two medevacs and extra 3600 miles had been to come in the top half of the 12-boat fleet.

Your sense of success very much ties in with your definition of success. If my goal had been to win the London Marathon or complete it in under four hours, then I would have been disappointed. However, my definition of success on this occasion was just to finish! And I did finish, despite "limp-walking" for the last seven miles, so I was able to celebrate that. With skiing to the South Pole, my definition of success was to finish at the South Pole, not just to see how far I could go, and this aim is what powered me through the painful days in the last two weeks. Other expeditions and adventures have had stretchy goals or at least expectations set by myself, and usually I have succeeded in meeting these criteria. Occasionally I haven't, for various reasons, and I have had to come to terms with that and learn from it. I know I am human and that failure is part of life, on condition that I have tried. My message to primary schools is: Give things a go, try very hard and then you will find we are more amazing that we realise.

So when we finished the Global Challenge, we had all given our best as a team and we danced into the final awards ceremony with our heads held high. We celebrated (got drunk) all over Portsmouth with our friends and families.

Then the hangovers hit us. Not just the post-drinking hangovers but the post-race blues. Over the next couple of days we returned to the boat to tidy up and gather our kit. Team members began leaving one by one. There were tears and hugs that went on and on over days as each crew member left to go home. We had been a tight team and we were disbanding. Then it was my turn to go. I first said goodbye to my bunk and carver box where I had kept all my kit. Even this rudimentary cloth bunk and plastic box at the back of the boat, which had seen such tough and difficult times, made me cry. I had lived here for ten months. I had sweated and slept, cried with laughter and anxiety, bumped and bruised, tossed and turned, dreamed and been woken to go on watch, three times a day, for nearly a year. That blue bunk and yellow box contained me while I was on board, and held ten months of my life forever. Crazy emotions for such inanimate, unattractive things - and then I had to say goodbye to my teammates! I was a blubbering wreck by the end. My sister and a friend were waiting to take me home and I don't think they could quite comprehend the huge rupturing and upheaval I felt inside. I think they were expecting me to skip off the damned boat and into the embrace of a warm and loving home.

The adventure was over. The organisers were packing up. The flags were coming down. The boat - MY wonderful, sturdy, secure, endearing, hardworking boat - was off on corporate charter. The team was breaking up. It was time to go.

I cried all the way home. My poor sister! I tried to stop but the tears kept flowing. My wonderful parents had slung a *Welcome Home* banner across the front of their house and I managed to be happy and genuinely excited to be back for a while. But then I went to London the next day to see a bunch of work colleagues who were playing Rounders on Clapham Common and I remember vividly standing outside Clapham Junction - where I had been hundreds of times before - trying to work out how to cross the busy road. I wasn't used to traffic and speed; I was not at all up to London pace yet. I stood there in a daze, probably through three or four traffic light changes; people must have thought I had lost the plot. My head was spinning.

My second memory was slowly walking towards the group of friends who I knew and loved so well, who I was dying to see, and just bottling it. I stood behind an oak tree hiding from them for a while. I wasn't sure I could face them all - so many of them and so suddenly. It was all a bit much. It had been a year since we last partied together to see me off. I eventually pulled myself together and sauntered out from behind the tree to greet them.

And then, weirdly, after a few minutes of "hellos" and "well dones" and hugs, I found myself sitting down with a small group of my old girlfriends and they weren't talking about sailing. They were talking about having babies... and I was miles away. They didn't understand my world and I was struggling to understand - or even care - about theirs. It felt very odd, and not at all how things should be. I felt distant and woolly. My friend Kelly had nailed it, I felt: *very flat, slightly depressed and had the feeling that everything was so insignificant here...*

After backpacking around the world, probably at an age when I was feeling most invulnerable - I wrote at the end of my diary: *Deep sadness of an adventure's end, excitement at the thought of seeing my family and home in about eight hours, and worry about my future.* I had been away for eight months, flip-flopping around, enjoying a lifestyle of backpacking and travelling, tolerant and open-minded, friendly and gregarious, relaxed and carefree, but then I came back home. From arriving at the airport, in flip-flops and a sarong, looking incredibly healthy, tanned and fit, with a scuffed backpack and souvenirs and a beatific smile, it took a couple of days to lose some of that serenity and peace, and start feeling slightly stressed, busy and self-centred again. You go to work, complain about the weather and then watch TV. I can understand why Moitessier kept sailing. He had found a spiritual existence on a higher plane.

On return from the South Pole, I was worried that the post-adventure blues would hit me twice as hard. The bigger the adventure, the greater the contrast to your everyday life, the harder you can fall on return. The adjustment both physically and mentally is immense. To transition from skiing every day in a fairly solitary manner, in a huge white frozen continent with no residents, no darkness and no wildlife, to landing at Heathrow among thousands and thousands of people with all the noise of the world's fifth busiest airport in the world... It was loud, confusing and chaotic.

Perhaps I was lucky that I was on quite strong drugs for my legs and that kept me peaceful! I was taking 12 Tramadol a day, notorious for making you relaxed and sleepy, plus I was on anti-depressants to keep my painful nerves calm, so I was slightly zoned out for the first few months of my return. I slept a lot. I drank many bottles of prosecco as people came to visit and congratulate me; it was actually one of the more pleasant homecomings. I was also desperately happy to be back home. Skiing to the South Pole had been the most gruelling, relentless adventure I had ever done. It had required physical effort all the way. I had lost 15 kilograms and was exhausted and in pain. It was time to hit the sofa.

I was cocooned and looked after, floating in a hazy world of fizz, Tramadol and anti-depressants. Maybe this is the best way to come down after a major expedition? (Please don't take me seriously on that point!) Alex and I also decided to treat ourselves to a luxury holiday. So my recipe to cure post-expedition blues is possibly:

1) 1 x very accommodating other half to pamper you
2) Heaped tablespoons of fabulous neighbours and friends who want to hear ALL about your trip IN DETAIL
3) A kilo of communication with the other travelling buddies to process thoughts and feelings
4) Time not working to relax, decompress, edit photos and videos
5) Several litres of champagne or Prosecco
6) 1 x holiday in the Maldives
7) A sprinkling of pills to keep you holding on to that zen-like state
8) Oh, and an idea about what your next adventure may be...

As I write, it's been a year since I went to Antarctica. A year since I gingerly stepped off the plane onto the ice, feeling "imposter syndrome" and waiting for a real adventurer to come along and take my place.

Last week I met up with my teammate Julian - now the headmaster of Wellington College, one of the best public schools in England. We sat in his expansive Master's Study, drinking tea out of a china cup and saucer, with a patterned plate of delicate biscuits. In front of me was a clean shaven man in a suit and in front of him was a girl in a dress and high heels with clean and coiffed hair. We had never seen each other looking like this and we felt out of context. I was used to Julian striding along on his skis, with his white headphones, reflective goggles and iced-up beard. He was used to me being slightly less graceful, bouncing along with pumped up music playing in my ears, dancing one minute and then moaning about my back the next. There is a classic piece of footage from when Julian interviewed me at the end of a day's sledging. He asks me how my day has been. I'm lying exhausted on my pulk, totally spent, with my eyes shut, and back in agony. I open my eyes, look into the camera, and say that it was a great day and that I could do it all again. The twinkle in my eye and Julian giggling in the background says it all.

As we sat in his plush office, suited and booted, we reminisced about the good, the bad, and the ugly. A year gave us perspective. We had turbulent emotions on the anniversary of our departure and had been absorbed in the social media build up to this year's season: the clearing of the blue-ice runway; the first flight of the Ilyushin from Punta Arenas; setting up camp at Union Glacier; watching the key players who were going to be skiing this year... It brought back vivid memories, and made us content and sad to recollect.

With no doubt we were both extremely pleased and proud of what we had achieved, not just getting to the South Pole, but getting there with a certain degree of style, fortitude and civility. We both acknowledged that there had been issues, but that we had maintained a positive attitude. Despite the cruelty of the circumstances and the occasional indignity of what we had to do and help each other with, we held on to our values and integrity. Pain is temporary, pride is forever. We had learned a lot. For me, I got a confirmation that the positive qualities I had were better and stronger than ever. I was satisfied with how I had carried myself, from the first tyre pulling and training in Norway to the agony and ecstasy of the South Pole arrival. *"To strive, to seek, to find, but not to yield."*

I like to reflect after an adventure. Some experiences need time to mature like a good wine, allowing thoughts and feelings to ripen. Time gifts us with perspective and wisdom. When I speak at a school or conference, I get asked questions - weird, funny, personal and deep questions - which make me examine myself to find the right and honest answer, and it's when I falteringly share my insights that the audience lean in and really get it. Stories about the fine line between resilience and quitting; stories about fear and vulnerability; stories about savouring, seizing, loving life, going for it, stretching, digging deep, stepping up, embracing the mess, living and dying.

It is sometimes when we are close to death that we feel fully alive. Sometimes the frailty or finality of life provokes us to fully live. We don't want to be lying on our deathbeds regretting all the things we haven't done. Life is an adventure, and adventure is living.

Full Circle

I had a friend called Jon Scott who died recently of throat cancer. He was a Marine. A tough guy who ran marathons right up to the end for Cancer Research and Macmillan. He left behind him a young wife and three children. On the wall in their kitchen is a list of "100 Happy Days" which they created together while Jon was alive to give the family something positive to do together after his passing. Sometimes these awful circumstances are the catalyst for us deciding to do some great things with our lives. 100 Happy Days.

How many days do we live? 30,000? Let's make them worthwhile. Let's live life to the full.

Philosophies

In alphabetical order, here are my top mantras or philosophies to support Living Life to the Full:

Be fearless. We all get scared; it's how you cope that matters. Embrace the fear and do it anyway.

Choose your Attitude. You can choose to be fearful and worried and limited and unable, or you can choose to challenge yourself and step up. You can be constructive, positive and re-motivated by a crisis, or negative, despondent and finger-pointing. One makes you feel better, one doesn't. One has energy for moving on, one doesn't.

Dig Deep. It's when we are at the hardest, darkest, steepest part of the journey that we most want to call it a day. But this is when you find your deepest, strongest, most incredible willpower. When you have to dig deep, you will find there is more depth of resource within you. There are reserves of energy and determination that lie buried within us, but they are there. They are there when we really need them, when it really matters.

Don't set out to fail. Set out to finish. If you set out with potential failure in your head, then this will become your construct and you will try less, do less and achieve less. Set out to finish or win.

Embrace the Mess. Not only go with the flow, but enjoy the ride. Life is messy, embrace it.

Give it 100% commitment. No half-hearted efforts, if you're going to do something, do it to the best of your ability with your whole heart, body, mind and soul. Raise your game.

Give things a go. Don't hesitate or procrastinate. Take a leap.

Give yourself positive beliefs and positive labels. If we think we can, we can; if we think we can't, we won't. We have positive and negative beliefs about ourselves, and the negative beliefs or labels will limit us and the positive ones will set us free. Limiting beliefs will affect your confidence and whether you go for it or not. I couldn't sail. So what? I learnt! All the time you are using limiting beliefs and applying limiting labels you won't do these things, because you think you can't. But you know what? You can, and then you will. The more positive beliefs you have and the more positive labels you give yourself, the more free you will be to do what you want.

If the will is there, then there is a way. There is only one thing stopping you from achieving your goals, and that one thing is yourself; if you are determined enough to succeed, then you will. And if the will is there, then the way can be found.

Just do it. Go for it. Don't think about it too hard, don't weigh up the pros and cons, and don't get tangled up in knots ruminating or held down with hundreds of inhibitive ties. Just do it. Make it happen. No regrets. Take the leap, the leap liberates us from our limits. Leaping takes courage, *just doing it* takes courage, but the big stuff needs courage, otherwise it wouldn't be big. Teetering on the edge, or taking small steps, doesn't get you across the chasm between where you are now and where you want to be.

Live Life to the Full. Make your life extraordinary by living it fully, heartily and happily. Embrace life. Enrich it with adventures, achievements, experiences, memories, wonder and magic. In order to fully live we must live life to the full. Life is an adventure and adventure is life.

Look Forward, Not Down. Learn from the past, look to the future and live in the present. Learn and grow from previous experiences and build that toolbox, knowledge bank and resilience for future use. Be future focused and look forward to living; aim for where you want to be. Look Forward - have goals, ambitions, aspirations and dreams; plan ahead and prepare thoroughly for the adventures to come, and keep your head up; be alert and stay positive.

Manage the Pain, Manage the Brain. When you have a physical illness or injury, don't just manage the physicality of it, also manage what is going on inside your head - your psychology. Focus on making them *both* better. When you feel mentally healthier, you will feel much happier overall and research has shown that this may aid your physical recovery.

Pain is Temporary, Pride is Forever. Behave always in a way that will make you proud - for always. Even if you are tired, or in pain, or just lacking the energy, these things are temporary. Your achievement will last forever.

Seize the Day, Savour the Moment. We can choose to seize or savour (or both) depending on our age, mood, energy or goals. Grab life by the horns as well as stop to appreciate it. Live both boldly and keenly, go for it and delight in it, live in the present and be present, do more and be more... Be stretched and challenged, edgy and hedonist, as well as peaceful and awestruck, nurtured and eudaemonic.

Step Up, Don't Give Up. Listen to your **Don't Quit Tigers.** The Give-up Gremlins are very persuasive, but the solution is usually to step up, not give up. To rise to the challenge, dig deep, feel the fear and do it anyway. This uphill path, or this choice, is tougher, yet ends at a higher finishing place. A place of accomplishment, pride, fulfilment, confidence and gratification that will stay with you forever. We are made of strong stuff, boys and girls, men and women. Not sugar and spice or snails and puppy dog tails, but resilience, fortitude, determination, hope, courage, grit and guts.

Stretch. If we stay in our comfort zone we will learn less, be less capable and skilled, less wise and experienced, and the more stuck we will be in our safe, controlled place. The more you stretch mentally, physically, spiritually and emotionally, the more alive, motivated, focused, and sharp you will feel.

We are all more amazing than we realise. And more capable.

What is your point of reference? When you are thinking of giving up, what do you think about? Think about all the times you HAVE coped, you have made it through, you have got to the finish without quitting, this is what is going dominate your head and feed your thoughts. This success becomes your anchor.

Thanks

Alex Alley for supporting me in everything I do. Good luck with your solo, non-stop, round-the-world record attempt Alex! www.alexalley.com.

My mum and dad who have enabled me to be who I am, do what I do and live life to the full.

Belinda Kirk and Explorers Connect for inspiration. www.explorersconnect.com.

Julian Thomas for being such a great South Pole buddy.

Helen Turton for making me believe I could. www.newland.no.

Jennifer Barclay for editing. jennifer-barclay.blogspot.co.uk.

Pauline for proofreading and Buzz Erlinger-Ford for inspiring the cover design.

A special mention

To my chosen charity - Gutsy Gastros - supporting children and teens with life-long, life-threatening and life-limiting bowel conditions. www.justgiving.com/gutsygastros.

Get in Touch

For talks, workshops, coaching or conversation:

www.paula@paulareid.com

@ThePaulaReid

ThePaulaReid

WS - #0029 - 051121 - C0 - 216/138/10 - PB - 9781784563899 - Gloss Lamination